Pause and Decide

Pause and Decide
A Mindful Approach to Everyday Decisions

Evangeline Brooks

Mindful Pages

Published in 2025

ISBN: 9789362923561 (PB)
ISBN: 9789362922700 (eBook)

Published by

Mindful Pages
Imprint of Alpha Editions LLC
312 W. 2nd St #1834
Casper, WY 82601, USA
www.mindfulpagespublishers.com

All rights reserved. No part of this publication may be reproduced, distributed, or transmitted in any form or by any means, including photocopying, recording, or other electronic or mechanical methods, without the prior written permission of the publisher, except in the case of brief quotations embodied in critical reviews and specific other non-commercial uses permitted by copyright law.

Contents

Introduction vii

1. The Foundation of Mindful Decision-Making 1

2. Cultivating Self-Awareness for Clarity 15

3. Developing Patience in Decision-Making 24

4. Staying Present to Make Informed Choices 31

5. Managing Stress and Anxiety in Decisions 36

6. Building Confidence in Your Choices 43

7. Mindful Decision-Making in Relationships 50

8. Applying Mindful Choices to Major Life Decisions 58

9. Embracing a Life of Clarity and Presence 65

About the Author 68

Introduction

The modern world is overwhelming with new advances in technology, a fast-paced lifestyle, and an abundance of information we are bombarded with every day, making a good decision be one of the most powerful things in the world. A present reality: we are confronted by countless choices, small and large, that lead us down a path one way or another, that ultimately decide our fate. But in the hustle of life, how often do we even stop to contemplate all the decisions we make, How many times do we do what we want with complete consciousness of our values and long-term strategic objectives with the potential harm to our well-being? This book takes the reader through a journey on how to make mindful decisions; a practice that allows us to face our decisions with clarity, patience and purpose.

While practice makes perfect, mindful decision making is not just about slowing down — but rather an awareness that creates a space in which we can see each choice as it really is, unaffected by the haze stress, anxiety or fight-or-flight reactions create. Decision making mindfulness is a muscle you can build and grow, one that causes pause, and thought and cause and effect, instead of reaction and counterreaction. In this opening chapter, we will touch on the significance of mindful decision-making, the common mistakes, often resulting in hasty or emotional decision-making and what the reader can expect to achieve by following along on this journey.

Mindful Decision Making: The Journey

It is a process of getting to know yourself, of practicing self-control; it is a journey of mindfulness in which you come to understand your mind. There is much more to this journey than making improved choices; it will change all the ways we think, feel, and act towards the world. Mindfulness, at its heart, means simply noticing what is happening at any moment, being aware of our thoughts and feelings as they are, without judgement or resistance. It expands our decision-making potential as when we practice mindfulness we start to gain the perspective to make decisions with utmost clarity and intention, thus opening a mental space to choose what best resonates with our core.

It is challenging, and the challenge can also be rewarding but it in itself is also a journey. It calls us to have a look at our routines, our knee jerk reactions, and the countless ways in which we may have been opting out of fear, lust for convenience or societal pressure. It is a journey that will force you to discover top qualities of growth, humility, and bendability. It is through the practice of mindful decision making that we start to liberate ourselves from the shackles of ancestral conditioning and step into an intentional, purposeful life. This is not about any immediate fix, rather a slow progression towards being more aware, being more in the now, being stronger within yourself, and all of this will create a better life.

Mindfulness and its role in decision making

Mindfulness is a word commonly tied to meditation, relaxation, and de-stressing. Mindfulness is more than these practices; it is a state of being that requires us to be present to the moment, to pay attention to what we are doing, our feelings and thoughts, elegantly noticing without judgment. Mindfulness in decision-making makes a decision-making process much more calm, clear, and insightful. We grow less responsive, more contemplative, and more capable of looking at the totality of a circumstance prior to making a decision.

Mindfulness as Decision Making Tool Mindfulness — powerful in the context of decision-making for multiple reasons. One, it allows us to see the emotions and backgrounds that may be affecting our decisions. We each possess an unconscious pattern to some degree; it could be avoidance of conflict, seeking approval, or making around snap decisions under stress. However, with mindfulness we observe these inclinations, and we are able to choose based on our genuine values instead of superficial feelings or social expectations.

In addition to that, mindfulness lets us make gut decisions open to possibilities. We can examine all sides and not feel compelled to jump to conclusions or stick with our first impressions. But such openness is often essential in being able to make the well-informed, nuanced decisions that these complex situations often require; the way forward is rarely obvious. It is simply about making decisions with a calm mind, without fear, without knowing what to do, trusting that the answers will come, simply by taking the time to explore our choices thoroughly instead of rushing.

Overview Of Mistakes Most Impulsive Or Stress-Driven Choices

Even if we have the best of intentions, most of us tend to choose in haste or out of stress. The word choice might be "react" instead of "respond" — It a band aid that can fade but we will be left empty and sometimes with guilt after discovering that our action will leave mark on us, and others. In high-pressure circumstances, we feel overloaded and are simply attempting to make things right so stress-driven choices abound. In times like these, it takes on excessive ease to make decisions that bring instantaneous relief, only to discover that they add to the hassle in the years to come.

Perhaps the biggest fallacy of a spur-of-the-moment decision is the path led by instant pleasure rather than long-term objectives. We might decide to buy something to make us feel better about stress, only to create financial stress later. Or, we may acquiesce to an obligation that we do not actually wish to take on, just to evade letting a different person down. These snap decisions are often made in the same breath recognizing that we do not really know what we need beyond the surface level, because we have never taken the time to realize this and discover ourselves, and they end up feeling empty or even hurtful with time.

Also, decisions made in stress are usually made out of fear or anxiety. When you are stressed out, your brain enters a simple survival mode, tightening the focus and restricting the full functioning of your thinking ability. When in this state, we may lose sight of the important, minimize possibilities, or fail to recognize the actual consequences of our decisions. Recognizing these unconscious tendencies offers an invitation to consider what conscious decision-making would do to transform these conditioned behaviours and how it can serve us at an optimal long-term level.

What Readers Will Get from This Book And

As readers dive into the pages of this book, they will find techniques, insights and tips for becoming a more mindful decision-maker. This book offers no quick solutions or instant fixes; instead it offers a path to a way of thinking that can be included in every part of your life. With each chapter you will learn pragmatic exercises, real-life stories, and contemplation questions to solidify your learning about mindfulness and how it can transform your decision-making process.

This book helps people recognize and work with their feelings in their decision making process so they can respond rather than react. They will learn ways to root themselves in the here and now, helping them feel some inner peace when things get chaotic. Through this book, readers will also have a better understanding of the mental shortcuts and hidden factors that could be influencing their preferences, enabling them to make choices that reflect their deepest beliefs and desires.

In conclusion, together with the book, you are accompanied on their path towards mindful choices and references, advice, and moral support are laid out as stepping-stones in the process. Ultimately, readers will be better equipped to face moments of choice with more awareness, intention, and wisdom over the course of the journey. They will be prepared to make choices that bring them external success and a genuine sense of inner peace and fulfillment.

The first chapter lays the ground for what is to come. The next chapters will elaborate on the practices, principles, and perspectives that make mindful decision-making a way of life. Every decision we have becomes a chance to be mindful, to make choices in line with our values, and to steer ourselves toward the life we want to lead. Now, as you flip the page and move on to the next chapter, know this journey is not just about choosing better—it is about becoming more mindful, more durable and more real than ever before.

1
The Foundation of Mindful Decision-Making

Given that, in our all-too-original world of choices, there seem to be more choices to be made more frequently than breaths taken, mindful decision-making may well be the North Star. But what is mindful decision making, really? It is the kind of decision-making that transcends logic, pros and cons lists, and snap judgments. At its most basic, mindful decision-making is being conscious and purposeful in each decision, in a way that your actions align with your value and, longterm goals. Mindful decision-making, on the other hand, is a deliberate, considered process that allows us to reflect on how we want to respond, and on what effect our decision will have on us, on others and the environment compared to ordinary decisions made in autopilot or haste.

Definition and Purpose

Mindful decision-making is based on the principles of mindfulness, which is being present, or in other words, observing the moment without judgment. It reminds us to pause, assess, and respond from a place of not automatic reaction or following societal expectations, but from a nuanced awareness of who you are, what you want, and what is happening around you. And: by practicing mindful decision-making, we try to make choices that align more closely with who we actually are and create more peace and meaning in our lives.

Mindful decision-making is about more than just the avoidance of mistakes or actions we may regret. And yes, these are great side effects, but the real intention is to help people live more consciously, creating a life that reflects what they really want and need. Mindful decision-making gives us the power to stop and think before we act, to understand why we feel compelled to choose one thing over another, and to align with our long-term lives. We learn to listen more closely to ourselves, and to feel confident in our decisions, following paths that suit us individually, rather than simply whatever whim comes to mind next, or whatever plan we can gather from other people.

When one acts with intention in decision-making, he or she assumes the position of self-leadership, carefully crafting him or herself and his or her life. It helps us identify and diffuse knee-jerk reactions and emotional triggers, often based on prior effects, fears, or prejudices. No longer just spectators of our own lives, we become key players where we have the inner space to make conscious choices that honor our values, our well-being, and our fulfillment.

The everyday benefits of mindfulness

The advantages of practicing mindfulness as a filter for your decision-making process are limitless and will help you in ways that go far beyond a single decision, spurring benefits that impact your mental, emotional, and even physical health. Mindfulness helps to lower stress, increase concentration, develop emotional resilience and expand our capacity to connect with others and lead a happier, healthier and more meaningful life.

Reduced Stress One of the very first advantages of mindful decision-making is that you can relieve stress. When living in a world that seeks immediate response and rapid resolution, it can be daunting and anxiety-producing, particularly when making significant decisions. Being mindful will invite us to take a breather, take some deep breaths, and make decisions with a clearer mind. That serenity serves as a protective barrier against stress, clearness of thought that prevents rash anxiety-driven decisions. Mindful decision-making is how we apply the pause to decision-making, so rather than reacting due to stress, we can respond with more peace and clarity mentally in our decision making overall.

A good decision-making practice that mindfulness aids is greater concentration. Given all the distractions in this crazy world today, most of us find it hard to focus on one thought, one task at a time. We are constantly jumping from one idea to the next without fully investing in any of them! The practice of mindfulness cultivates the practice of attention — of focusing in on the present moment and grounding us in making each choice sit with us while we are present to experience it. It helps us deliberate the consequences as well as a multitude of paths available to all of us and finally act ourselves by following our rational minds and with the choices we make, we act in accordance to our best judgment. Eventually, this increased concentration leads to increased efficiency, making us more purposeful and capable in our work.

When we choose mindfully, we also build our emotional resilience, which is a key ingredient for handling life — and all of its difficulties. Decisions are full of emotions enthusiasm, anxiety, second-thoughts and regret. Mindful decisions allow us to notice these emotions instead of operating based on these thoughts. Awareness that allows us to then process our emotions in a positive way that keeps us steady and truly present even when things get hard. It helps us regulate our emotions and develop a sense of steadiness and adaptability such that we can weather the roller-coaster ride of life.

Moreover, mindfulness also improves our relationships by allowing us to communicate with empathy and compassion. A choice for some time with loved ones, or to settle a quarrel, or a decision to aid a confidant — decisions are frequently entangled with others. Practicing presence and compassion not only means we start to hear more closely what other people need, what their side looks like, and what we do in our relationships that honors that and what is called for in the name of care and non-harm. Awareness of the way we interact creates a greater connection between ourselves and those around us and increases the faith to connect with them through respect.

Making decisions with a mindful approach also helps us to ensure that our decisions lead to long-term well-being, as they are in harmony with our values and aspirations. Short-term satisfaction can often be derived from hasty choices, but few choices will fulfil you in the long run. Mindfulness reminds us that there is more than what we want right now: we must also think about how each decision works into the course of our lives with its many stories. Thinking this way allows us to act in ways that nurture our development, health and happiness in the long run. From career choices to lifestyle changes to the very act of setting goals, mindful decision making enables us to create a life that is not only purposeful but also sustainable.

Mindful decision-making is a practice that enables us to make our way through life more aware, intentional, and purposeful. It liberates us from reactivity, lowers the stress surrounding decision making, and enables us to live in accordance with our essence. Walking with words, as we do in this book, about mindful decision making from the mind of a man who has learned to transform into every moment, to find peace in every sensation, and deepen a relationship with all there is, from my own heart and yours. By making wiser choices, we are the architects of our own lives, creating a future in alignment with our most cherished values and dreams.

How Mindfulness Changes The Way You Make Decisions — The Science

Mindful decision making is about more than just awareness and calm, it has a tangible power. At its heart, it is all based in science that shows us, specifically, how mindfulness impacts our mind, our heart, and ultimately our behaviour. When we are mindful in our decisions, we activate certain circuits in the brain that enable us to think clearly, respond rather than react, and resist the pull of transitory impulses or stressors. When we explore the science surrounding mindfulness and how it can affect the way we make choices, we gain insight into why this practice is so powerful. In this chapter, we will look at what mindfulness does to our brain and emotions, and the difference between decision-making while stressed and calm.

NEUROPLASTICITY: What Are The Effects of Mindfulness on Brain and Emotion?

Mindfulness is not just a present state, but has immense structural and functional effects on the brain. There have been scientific studies in neuroscience in which suggest that regular practice of mindfulness alters the physical structure of the brain- those applies attention; regulates emotion, etc. It all starts in the brain where neural pathways are created that will become hardwired into our responses to life situations over time.

The prefrontal cortex — commonly known as the brain's "executive center" — is one of the major mind areas impacted by mindfulness. This brain region is associated with higher-order functions, such as reasoning, planning, and impulse control. When we practice mindfulness we fortify the prefrontal cortex to reflect, freeze-frame between stimulus and response, and to evaluate options against long-term consequences before we act. Mindfulness is building this region of your brain so that you make more intentional, thoughtful decisions as opposed to instinctual reactions! In a decision-making scenario, the prefrontal cortex is engaged and means that we examine the situation rationally—through the lens of our values and long-term objectives and not just the temporary whims or anxieties that try to manipulate us.

Yet another critical region influenced by mindfulness is the amygdalae, the brain's "alarm center" where responses to emotional stimuli (especially threats) are processed. During stressful, emotional situations the amygdala may engage more than the rational brain and a fight-or-flight response may override rational thought and more measured decision-making. When the amygdala hijacks the prefrontal cortex, all of those logical processes go out the window, and we often react impulsively. On the other hand, Mindfulness practice, regulates the work of amygdala, causes less amygdala reactivity and enables a cool and composed response from the individual in the situation. It does not imply that we stop having emotions; instead, we gain better control of our responses to these emotions, and we remain focused even on our peak stress points.

Mindfulness also helps the hippocampus which plays a role in memory and learning. Mindfulness supports the process of neurogenesis (the creation of new neurons) and keeps the hippocampus active and healthy, which leads to better memories of previously occurring situations that were successful or not in terms of how we made our choices. This better recall enables us to leverage past insights and lessons to inform our decision-making and to act in ways that are aligned with our goals and values.

Mindfulness also generates higher density grey matter, notably in regions of the brain associated with self-awareness/introspection and compassion. The shift in gray matter backs emotional intelligence, which allows us to understand our emotions and the reasons for our behaviour. The more awareness we have, the clearer we become about what we genuinely value and therefore, our choices become congruent with who we are. There you become aware of your capability to make decisions that could affect others thus being compassionate and empathetic; this encourages you to make ethical, considerate decisions.

Mindfulness here helps in creating emotional balance and equanimity. Mindfulness is when we witness our feelings objectively in the moment without trying to attach to them or being overly guided by them. This non-reaction to the situation enables us to view it objectively, ensuring that our judgement is not clouded by anger, fear, euphoria, or anything else. Mindfulness allows us to develop emotional balance, which enables us to make decisions on a cool, steady mind in the most difficult of moments. These are also part of emotional stability that help us make better decisions and also have benefits on our mental state and reduce stress anxiety and reactiveness in our normal life.

Decision-Making Under Stress versus Calm

While it might be significantly different making those same judgments under stress versus at ease. Under stress, both the body and mind lean toward reflex action instead of deliberative thinking; relief, not review. When you are stressed, the body releases hormones such as cortisol and adrenaline, making it prepared for agile response to an imaginary danger. This response is beneficial when the situation is life-threatening, however, this can cause poor decision making when the urgency context is where a thoughtful analysis is needed.

When we are stressed, the perspective of our brain shrinks thus cannot observe the big picture or it does not consider alternative paths. When we are under pressure, we tend to pay less attention to our surroundings and hone in on the task at hand, leading to a tunnel vision effect that predisposes us to make broad based decisions, can miss key details, and be unable to see long-term ramifications. Decisions made on impulse due to stress help to escape the feeling of discomfort, and a rather quick result mindset will put into place choices that relieve one in the short term with now focus on the underlying issue of this discomfort. An example might be someone who feels pressured to accept a job offer for a very high demanding position but ends up realizing that the role is not aligned with their values and long-term career goals. Stressful decision making will often choose the short-term gain over long-term fulfillment, which can leave us feeling regret or dissatisfaction.

However, using calm state decision making allows us to process information clearer and less biasness decisions are done by clearing our minds about short and long term results of our behaviour. Calmness turns on the prefrontal cortex, which allows us to process information in a more rational way and assess choices that do not involve emotion. By continuing to make more decisions from a place of calm, we can see the solutions that correlate with our values, we can reflect on experience, and we can anticipate the results of each possible decision. This helps us to make decisions aligned with our long-term well-being and overall mission in a way that results in a more meaningful and purposeful life.

Mindfulness is a practice that encourages a calm state of mind — it teaches us to observe our thoughts and emotions without reacting to them. Mindfulness teaches us to notice stress but not to act on it. It creates a mental "pause" that helps us view a situation objectively from a distance, rather than getting totally caught up in it; to take a step back instead and make solider choices from a space of clarity. Eventually, this pause becomes automatic which allows us to respond thoughtfully even under the highest level of stress.

Mindfulness also makes one more resistant to stress by lowering the physiological stress response. According to research, just being mindful decreases the cortisol level and reduces blood pressure, which lays a sense of relaxation and balances the level of tension hormones from stress. This calm in the body — in our physiology — is the perfect partner for a calm mind through mindfulness, allowing us to meet significant decisions with a balanced state of mind and body. Making decisions from this place of relaxation means we are much more likely to behave in a way that is best for us, resulting in a life that is reflective of who you truly are and what you truly want.

How mindfulness works explains its effectiveness in enhancing decision-making. Both things that all contribute to enhancing our ability to think clearly, manage emotional challenges, and be present in the present moment, by positively influencing the brain structure and function. What they found about decision-making under stress vs calm tells us how to tap into calm, mindful balanced states in our everyday life. These choices are often the ones that allow for a calm mind and awareness of the choice itself and the feeling behind it, interconnected.

It does not mean no stress or no hard decision-making. Rather, it is about cultivating the ability to meet these difficult moments with courage, insight, and mindfulness. In the next installments of this series, we will delve into concrete methods to weave mindfulness into our daily decision-making, laying the groundwork for a life driven by intention and greater fulfilment. Mindfulness allows us to recognize that we can drive what come after is not wrong or right, but decisions we make based on clarity and intention embodying all the decisions we have made to form the life we want, the life which reflects us as we are.

Acknowledging How You Make Your Decisions Currently

Every choice we make is a reflection of all the influences that got us there — our upbringing, personal values, previous experiences, and even unconscious bias. But many of us cruise through life on automatic, doing things without really noticing the patterns and habits that shape our decisions. Awareness of the way we astutely — the decision-making process — react is the beginning of a more conscious decision and more deliberate way of being. This chapter will cover a number of the more prevalent habits and biases that influence decisions, and it will offer exercises that will help you recognize your own decision-making style and the predictable patterns that you may not even realize exist.

Decision-Making: Common Habits and Biases

A natural impulses of human brain is taking shortcuts in thinking. Although this capacity for rapid cognition confers distinct evolutionary advantages such as fleeing before one realizes that there is a tiger chasing after her, it also makes us susceptible to acting impulsively, or even making arbitrary, biased, or pathologically risk-averse choices. These mental shortcuts, many of which are cognitively biased, can blind us, so that we fail to take in the whole picture and make decisions that do not support our goals or our values. Recognizing these biases and impulses is an important step toward escaping the more reflexive response and taking a more deliberate path to decision-making.

Confirmation Bias — As one of the most common decision-making diverges, confirmation bias happens when we look for information that confirms our previous beliefs or assumptions while ignoring those against it. If, for instance, they believe a specific diet does work for them, they are likely to only notice the success stories and ignore studies that go against that belief. This bias brings us narrow-mindedness, closing the option of seeing everything in an absolute way.

Overconfidence Bias: Overconfidence bias is the bias that leads employees to overestimate their knowledge, skills, or the accuracy of their forecasts. It can push us to gamble, over-guess, or overlook the downside. Things like confidence but more often it leads you to overconfident which results to making rash decisions but without nipping those important things in the bud. This bias awareness can help us stay humble in the presence of choice, opening doors for seeking feedback, different points of views.

1. Anchoring Bias — the idea that we anchor to the first data point. In other words, discovering that [a price] is not a good value is a shock two states away; if someone sees a product priced high, but then later sees it on sale, the person thinks the sale price is a lovely deal—even if it may still be more than what it is really worth. It can have an anchoring effect and make us unable to weigh options independently and make our decisions based on irrelevant reference points.

Loss Aversion: Loss aversion is the tendency to prioritize avoiding losses relative to acquiring gains, often driving people to make overly cautious or conservative decisions. Someone could, for example, miss out on a good investment opportunity due to the loss aversion that prevents them from spending money, even if the prospective upside is high. This kind of bias can stop us from making calculated risks or taking opportunities, because the fear of loss is the one that preoccupies our growth or success.

Status Quo Bias — The preference for continuation of a decision or state of affairs despite evidence showing a change has the potential for a better outcome. The habit that keeps us from moving forward, for example, is that we often feel reluctant to leave our safe zone or explore new offers. So, for instance, a person might be in a job they hate but the thought of making a change feels overwhelming so they just stay put despite the fact they would likely be happier elsewhere. Realizing this bias allows us a moment to work on acceptance of the change and open our mind and spirit to explore new avenues in life that are more in line with who we are.

Groupthink: As social beings, we are highly influenced by the decisions and views of others. Herd mentality is a phenomenon where people follow the crowd, especially in ambiguous situations. As much as social proof can be supportive, we can get lost in what we think others think, and stray away from what we value or need. When we notice ourselves doing this, we can start choosing to do something that represents our values instead of giving in to group think.

Instant Gratification: Many individuals are attracted to alternative options that give themselves an opportunity for immediate rewards, regardless of whether these options go against their long lasting goals or not. That penchant for instant gratification can result in choices that seem gratifying now, but hurt down the line. Saying no to something may feel good in the moment, say, procrastinating for a short time over a project that takes a long time to finish, but this can lead to stress and regret in the long term. By recognizing that we sometimes relive the past and live in the future, we can avoid making rash decisions that we may regret and instead make decisions that provide us with durable wellbeing.

We need to know about these biases and habits so that we can catch them when they start to affect our decision-making process. We need to find a level of awareness that helps us see the comforting patterns that no longer serve the purpose, and build up a new bandwidth of decision making on something that is so much more mindful and wholesome.

Activities to Recognize How You Make Decisions

In order to migrate toward mindful decision-making, you need to know what decision-making style you are using right now and how it is biased by experiences or default dispositions. These exercises are a way to think back on your own behaviors, find biases regarding people you may have and identify what influences the choices that you make. These exercises force you to look truthfully through your own decision-making and see places you can improve.

Decision-Making Journal

First step: Keep a decision diary for at least one week. Every single time you need to make a trade choice (large or little) simply make a note or more regarding the choice consisting of:

o What the decision was and the need for it.

o Your feelings leading up to, during, and following the decision.

This may involve: o The specific influences upon your decision, the people, thoughts etc.

o If you are happy with what happened or regret anything.

Take a look back to your journal entries after a week to find patterns. Find key themes or feelings found in all your choices. For instance, are you usually driven by loss aversion or sway easily by survival by consensus? This exercise raises awareness of sleeping habits and it can also highlight bias that might shape your decisions.

Reflecting on Major Decisions

What were three big decisions you made this past year? This could be in their choosing a career, relationship, financial investment, personal goals and so forth. To do this for each decision, ask yourself:

o What led you to make this decision?

o Did you look for advice or depending on information? If yes, from where did it originate?

o Were any of the familiar biases—confirmation bias, overconfidence, etc.—a factor?

o What were your feelings regarding the decision AFTER? Has your standpoint evolved overtime?

Reviewing the decisions of your past can help you to recognize which patterns and biases guide your behavior when making important decisions. This reflection both explains what is influencing your decisions and places you — along with your decision-making process — in a more mindful frame, suggesting where opportunities for improvement lie.

Breaking Down Choices, Small and Day to Day

Notice those everyday smaller choices going on in your response to the question: what do you want to eat, when do you want to go to work, what are you going to do in your free time. For any particular choice, ask yourself

o List two possible options for this decision — was it short-term gratification or long-term goal?

o Did you choose it because it was expedient, habitual or because you really wanted it?

How content are you with the outcome of the decision?

This exercise allows you to identify the patterns in your daily decision making. Recognising the choices you make out of habit or impulse allows you to begin transitioning toward even the smallest moments of collective decision-making with intention.

Pinpointing Your Go-To Decision-Making Approach

We have many different types of decisions we can make, and each style comes with its own strengths and weaknesses. Consider which one of these styles you are drawn to most frequently:

INTENT OPTIONAL: o Analytical: Do you need a large amount of information and information that you can analyze and dissect?

o Intuitive: Do you base your decisions primarily on gut feelings or instinctive reactions?

o Collaborative: Are you collecting input from others, making decisions by consensus or social support?

o Avoidant: Is your MO to defer decisions or avoid choices until you have to?

Understanding which style you like helps you understand the impact it has on your decisions. Consider if this style is working for you or if there are circumstances where a different style would be beneficial.

Buitoni, then, opts to draw the line at occasionally practicing mindfulness — meditation, in other words — as a way of forcing oneself to notice the brain's pre-decision impulses.

Mindfulness meditation practice for decision making You should find a quiet area, close your eyes and take a few deep breaths. Think of a recent decision, then notice what you are thinking and feeling about that decision. Observe possible tension, excitement or doubt, but do not judge. While you breath, think about the reason why you do this and ask yourself whether this is part of your long-term objectives or values. This meditation will help you tune into the deeper reasons for your choices, and bring more awareness into the way you make decisions.

Understanding how you make decisions today, is a critical starting point for taking a larger, more mindful operating principle to the rest of your life. When you realize the biases and habits which influence your decisions, you start understanding the influences behind your choices. The exercises in this chapter will encourage you to reevaluate your decision-making style, reveal unconscious habits, and start the process toward more conscious choices.

Keep in mind that the purpose of mindful decision-making isn't to eradicate every bias or habit, but rather to notice when either of those is influencing your choices so you can choose for yourself. So as you explore more about mindful decision-making, keep this information handy. It brings about recognition of your patterns which leads to change, helping you make choices more clearly, rationally, confidently and with alignment with your values. Every choice is a gateway, and with consciousness, you can make each choice part of you, and get closer to a better, more mindful life.

2

Cultivating Self-Awareness for Clarity

A meaningful life is built on values and priorities. Morals are an internal compass that guides our actions, decisions, and ultimately, the path we take. This knowledge of what we value and prefer encourages us to make better decisions that can satisfy our lives as well as our real selves. Here, the chapter considers the importance of identifying your core values and discovering, through exercises, those values that serve to build a life representative of who you are.

But before you start, you first need to understand what are core values. These are the beliefs that shape our values and our behavior, our attitudes, and ultimately how we choose to see the world. Core values are the values we practice the most and are the values we hold dear and find meaning. These differ per individual, but values such as honesty, integrity, respect, compassion, and responsibility are common. Those are the traits that make us experience well-being and purpose when we incorporate them into our lives.

It is sufficient for three reasons to be aware of your core values. They guide you on what decisions you need to make first. Core values provide a filter to help assess alternatives, ensuring that the choices we make are in line with who we genuinely are. This alignment develops self-integrity, as we are less likely to behave in harmful ways that oppose our beliefs, leading to self-respect and confidence. Moreover, how we behave according to our values impacts the way others see us which in turn gives us our reputation and deepens our connections with others.

In addition, being clear about our values strengthens resilience. Further, in moments of struggle, individuals who have clarity around their values can also hold on to these as a foundation to keep them centred and motivated. When our actions reflect our values it brings less internal conflict and strife as we do not make contradicting choices to our beliefs — that is experiencing inner peace. We also live in alignment with our values — and that is where peace and authenticity come from.

Core values are revealed through self-analysis and through a practice of introspection. After all, many values maybe even most, exist further down in our psyche and may not always be visible or verbalized. Identifying and defining these values has the potential to be transformative, and serves as a foundation for decision making and actions which are in alignment with our true selves.

After we clarify what our values are the next thing to do is make sure all actions and decisions actually match them. This alignment is such an important part of purpose-driven living (which encompasses self-reflection, boundary-setting, and goal-setting practices). We could start reminding ourselves from time to time whether our choices reflect our values and change them where necessary. This may require the establishment of boundaries; avoiding situations or people that challenge or diminish our values to maintain interactions and contexts that build us up rather than break us down.

Further, it is important that we set objectives aligned with our values. Values-based goals are more impactful and sustainable to maintain because they are aligned with our values. When we make decisions mindfully, we check each choice against how we want to live our lives, small and large, which helps us prioritize and make sure our decisions reflect what matters most to us. This is why my decisions always come from a place of authenticity and insight, and they always flow effortlessly from who I am.

There are numerous exercises that can aid in this process, helping to elucidate our values and solidify this abstract concept in our minds. An engaging methodology is the list of values sorting activity. Get a List of Common Values — Loyalty, Independence, or Compassion Go through this list and choose the ten that resonate the most with you and hone in on five that are a core part of your identity. Think about why these values are significant to you, and identify moments in your life when those values influenced your decisions or behavior.

One other useful exercise is the reflection on peak experiences. Read back on times you have felt so fulfilled or peaceful and take note of what you were doing, who you were with, and what made that experience so meaningful. Take a moment to think about any recurring themes or traits that all of these experiences have in common. And sometimes, these instances uncover values that are very important to us and that have a high degree of impact in our lives.

Thinking about role models is another important one. Think of people, fictional or otherwise, whom you admire — whether they're relatives, companions, iconic figures, or famous faces — and write down what it is you like about them. If you take these characteristics of your best leaders and compare them against your first list of values, it can show you values you may want to include, exclude or reorder. The characteristics in others that we most value are, more often than not, the characteristics we possess that we cherish, or the characteristics we would like to possess.

Here is a big one — the eulogy exercise. Consider the end of your life and a eulogy being read about you. Consider how you'd like people to talk about you and the words or phrases you'd like to be ascribed. The words beneath these values often embody the attributes you hold most dear, defining the legacy you want to leave behind.

A daily reflection journal is also a great tool to integrate your values awareness into your life. Take some time at the end of the day, to see how you fulfilled your values. Alternatively, take note of moments where you felt aligned with your values, and moments where you felt out of alignment. You will start to see patterns over time, giving clues to where your values are truly reflected in your life and where they are not.

Third, conflicts analysis can provide lessons in values. Consider some of the disagreements from this past year, what values were on the line there? Usually, conflicts arise when we feel that our values are being threatened or when we perceive that the other person is behaving oppositely to our beliefs. Knowing what these situations involved on the values-level can give much clearer insight about our deepest priorities, and may illuminate values we would do well to grow or change.

Ultimately, knowing your values and priorities is a lifelong process of listening, reflecting, and recalibrating. As life happens and the seasons change, we might find that what we value involves different colour for each season, so checking back in with this exercise every few years is a good reminder to keep the integrity of yourself intact. Knowing our core values helps us prioritize, make better decisions, and lead a life that is true to us. This alignment creates a sense of completeness and calmness, and gives us the power to live in accordance with our greatest values.

Recognizing (Your) Emotional Triggers

Emotions are super strong movers of what we do, how we act, and the choices we make — and they do not always come from our heads. Emotions always have a role to play — they can enhance our experiences and teach us meaningful lessons about ourselves, but they can also cause us to act impulsively or foolishly if not properly understood and kept in check. Identifying our emotional triggers is actually an important step in understanding how emotion can drive our decisions. Recognizing these triggers and understanding how to control them will give you the tools to allow your emotions to be productive, engaging with them to make decisions based on what you really want and represent.

Triggers are things, words, memories, or people that provoke a reaction. These reactions are built over time through exposure to past experiences, personal beliefs or lingering fears and desires. For example, if someone was previously punished for criticizing someone, that person might feel immediate rage when someone else criticizes them. Another individual may feel profound sorrow or anxiety when in circumstances that trigger memories of past losses. These triggers affect our perspective and reaction to events and situations where we need to think clearly instead of impulsively reacting and regretting about the bad decisions we make. Understanding these feelings and the circumstances that trigger them is the basis of awareness and emotional intelligence.

This understanding of which emotions influence our choices gives us valuable insight into our individual patterns. For instance, when you see that anger is causing you to a react and make aggressive or defensive choices, you know that in those situations, you need to be on the ball. Likewise, if you detect emotions like fear, jealousy or any form of insecurity, this can serve as a cue to stop and think before you make a choice, as one will more likely act on impulse unintentionally rather than in a rational manner. When you observe these patterns, you get the chance to control your emotional reactions, guiding you on how to decide according to your objectives and principles rather than those influenced by ephemeral emotional states.

Once you are aware of the emotional triggers that effect you, the following step is to implement techniques to regulate these feelings. And all the different tools we can use to respond instead of react to our feelings. A strong method of this is mindfulness (which is the practice of watching your emotions without judgment). So when you look at an emotion — anger for example or sadness — without attaching a label that says "bad," you create a psychological gap that enables you to contemplate what your answer will be rather than just being impulsive. Mindfulness teaches you to notice when emotions show up with out being consumed by the feelings and responds because they are intentional and thoughtful.

Another useful technique for how to relax emotional triggers is to do deep breathing exercises. Feelings, particularly strong ones, can trigger physical reactions like faster heartbeats, rapid breathing, or muscle tension. Slow, deep breaths can trigger the body's relaxation response, which opposes the physiological effects of stress; generate a slow, steady flow of blood to the brain and relax the body and mind. This change in the body allows for clearer thought, allowing for the ability to view the situation with logic rather than emotionally. When having a difficult conversation, breathing might help in the sense that, instead of responding in defense, you take a few breaths, calm yourself down to respond back.

Also, reframing your thoughts is great for handling emotional triggers. Reframing is the conscious act of presenting a situation in a more positive (or neutral) light. If constructive criticism sends you into a tailspin, for instance, reframing allows you to use that feedback as a chance to improve rather than as a personal insult. This change in how you perceive it can reduce the emotional power behind the response and create a healthier mindset that allows you to respond in a way that is aligned with what you know is in your best interest long-term.

Another method to understand your emotional triggers is to journal. When you write about emotions, you process and reflect on your feelings and discover the logical reasons for your responses.

Journaling helps you see patterns of thought and behavior, and discover common triggers to extreme emotions. When we know what these triggers are, we are better able to predict the emotional response and plan meaningful and constructive methods to address that response when it occurs.

When it comes to managing emotional triggers, visualization exercises can be an important part of the process. If you visualize a challenging situation occurring and you being calm, over time you become less shy about facing that challenging situation in real life. Using visualization to prepare for potential emotional triggers allows you to develop your resilience to these types of situations and makes it easier for you to stay calm in scenarios that may have otherwise drawn out an intense emotional response.

In short, identifying emotional triggers — and learning how to keep them in check — is an art (and science) of self-exploration and practice. Once you are aware of what triggers your emotions, identifying emotions in the moment will become easier and you will start to make decisions that are less influenced by a temporary emotional experience and more aligned with your fundamental values and goals in life. And this awareness and management of emotions leads to more balanced, measured, and rewarding decision-making, empowering you to use your emotions as a force for good in your life.

Awareness: Mindfulness Exercises To Practice

Mindfulness is simply being aware of the present moment, in a nonjudgmental way. Mindfulness exercises can improve awareness of thoughts, feelings and physical sensations, helping a person write a thoughtful response to the demands of life rather than a hysterical reply. When we're mindful, we are more aware and have self-awareness, helping you face everyday challenges like a calm water and clear mind. In this chapter, you will find some guided exercises to reflect and be present with even a few daily practices in your life to bring more self-awareness.

The first step of mindfulness is presence, a trait that you can actually train by using guided exercises that teach you how to observe your feelings and thoughts in the moment, as they are. For example, one type of exercise is called the body scan, where we move the mind through each body part from head to toe, paying attention to sensations and feelings without trying to change anything. Find a quiet spot, sit or lay comfortably, close your eyes and pay attention to your breath as it moves slowly. Starting from the top of your head, work your way down through your body and look for any areas where you may be tense, feeling pain, or heat. This approach allows you to locate spots where there is physical tension, but it also encourages deep relaxation as you give all of your attention to each part of the body and breathe stress away.

Mindful breathing (observing the natural flow of your breath) Mindful breathing is another powerful mindfulness exercise. Sit comfortably in a chair, close your eyes, and focus on every breath you take in and out. Don't try and control the breath, just pay attention to it, even how it feels, how quickly or slowly you are breathing and how deep you may be breathing. Mindful breathing grounds you in the present when life gets hectic or feels overwhelming. This practice actually also cultivates awareness of how often your mind wanders; wherever your thoughts take you, gently bring the focus back to the breath. With time, mindful breathing turns into a manner to center your self while stress knocks on the door.

Mindfulness meditation allows thoughtful self-awareness through observation without attachment, deeply reflecting internally. Take five minutes every day to sit up straight and still, close your eyes, and allow your mind to just exist. When the thoughts come, let them come, observe them as if watching clouds pass in the sky rather than shoving them away. Watch each thought arise nonjudgmentally, whether a memory, a worry, an image, irrespective of what it is. You can discover the limits of your thinking, and understand how the thought motivates a feeling. Mindfulness meditation creates less reactivity, and more room in the head for peacefulness, which you are then able to cultivate further and respond to what life throws your way with greater equanimity over time with practice as you respond rather than reacting.

Along with much more structured and guided exercises, these small, simple practices can certainly have action in self awareness and help you maintain awareness during the day. For example, every morning,

I set an intention. Spend a couple of minutes at the beginning of your day and think of how you would like to live it: with patience, with gratitude, with courage. Whatever your intention is say it out loud or in your mind—as you go about your day carry it with you as a touchstone. That makes you mindful of your actions and your reactions and grounds you in behaviour that is intentional, presence driven – that grounds you in purpose.

Another daily mindfulness practice that may be useful is to practice mindful walking. PAYING ATTENTION TO EVERY STEP AS YOU WALK SOONEST WE WILL FEEL YOUR FEET REACHING TO GROUND AND OUR BODY MOVES During this moment of practice you should focus on your surroundings — what colors, sounds, and smells are surrounding you without focusing your mind upon your worries or responsibilities. When you immerse yourself in the experience of walking, you strengthen your capacity to stay in the present and observe what you might miss out on in the busyness of life. This way, mindful walking turns an ordinary walk into a calming and transformative practice by clearing the mind.

Keeping a gratitude journal is another effective method of using mindfulness to become more self-aware. Finally, at the end of each day, write down at least three things that you are grateful for, no matter if they are highlights or simple little things. Gratitude helps you notice really good things in life, which puts your life into perspective and creates a sense of resilience and happiness. If you take some time to look back over these moments of gratitude, this helps you take a look at what is most important to you and how to adjust your life to match these values.

Mindfulness is also about being available with other people, which For example, active listening can improve relationships and increase self-awareness. If you are talking to someone just listen to your conversation with them, not what you say next or ponder. Listen to their tone of voice, body language, and facial expression; give your full attention to their best. This allows you to be present and more mindful in your interactions with each other and yourself, providing the space to reflect on how can you engage with others.

The mindfulness exercises and practices mentioned above cultivate awareness when we incorporate them into our daily routines.

Mindfulness is a way to practice with lay time so you can become more sensitive to your thoughts, emotions, and surroundings. That will become something that you can make decisions from a centered calm conscientiousness that connects your actions to your values and intentions. Even if only sometimes for five minutes a day, these actions help inspire a mindful way of living that brings you more presence, peace and insight into your true self into your life.

3

Developing Patience in Decision-Making

The art of pausing is a superpower in when we live in a world that is always pressuring us to do something, react, make a split second decision, we can learn to create lucidity and agency. Decision forging is the practice of pausing prior to a choice, giving us the opportunity to breathe, reflect, and respond in ways that are in line with our values and goals versus responding on impulse. By giving ourselves time to slow down before we make a decision, we can see some massive benefits, from improving our ability to make well-considered choices, to reducing impulsive behaviors that may cause regrets that result in more actions being taken.

There are so many good reasons to slow down before making a decision. When we slow down, we allow ourselves to consider the many possibilities before us. It opens a gap where we can digest the ramifications of every option, where we can predict the downstream effects — both good and bad. However, if we are angry or triggerable — we must slow down just to step out of an emotionally reactive place. A lot of this stems from emotion, and often times we make decisions influenced by our emotions that we would otherwise not make — which we might come to regret. When we pause, there is a space between our emotions and our reactions, where we get context and clarity and what is most important.

Furthermore, when we slow down (pause), we can access our intuition more deeply. Amidst the thermal hurry to establish conclusions, we often sideline the quiet wisdom, the intuition perhaps, that might lead us somewhere. When we pause we tune in, to those softer, generally wiser, internal audible signals. This link with our guiding spirit ensures that the choices we make which appear suit our lives are also aligned with our true selves. In the long run, the practice of pausing may enable us to respond to life from a place of intuitiveness and mindfulness, where the decision comes from a place of an inner bright spot where we are quiet.

Part of understanding the value of taking a pause is identifying impulsive urges as well. Stress, excitement, or a high emotional state usually activates the impulse. This feels like an impulse that prompts us to act right away without thinking through the implications of our actions. Examples range from the desire to react immediately when engaging in an argument, through to the impulse to purchase something we did not plan for, or to agree to more commitments than we have capacity for. When we recognize these moments in real time, we become more in tune with how impulsive desires manifest for us. The first step to managing these urges is awareness: being aware of this feeling allows us to exercise some willpower when we need to.

Impulsivity is very often permanent in nature that the DESIRE to resolve an UNCOMFORT related with impatience, discomfort, and or NEEDS DEEPLY request fast solution. So when we feel anxious or under pressure, we may do things irrationally to try to feel in control or to have the certainty of knowing that we did everything we could. However, an idea that pops into your mind will seldom serve you for long and should be addressed cautiously as this may create other issues. Pausing, conversely, is the place we can reside for at least a moment in the discomfort and think of better channels for its expression. That small gap is all it takes to change your viewpoint, which might present new possibilities that would be overlooked in a reactionary moment.

Incorporating stopping into the fabric of our everyday routines helps us to become more patient and, in turn, have more room for tolerating uncertainty. For the enhancement of responding instead of reacting, we need to use pausing successfully, which will help us to handle challenging circumstances calm and focused. The more we practice pausing the more we notice our own blueprints and triggers. This makes us develop emotional intelligence to know when we are operating on impulse or intention.

Ultimately, stopping before deciding is an easy, powerful practice with a ton of benefits. The mind has more insight and can align choices at its will, and thereby minimizes the opportunities for capricious decision-making, while also enabling more emotional identification. Cultivating the practice of pausing helps us to become intentional and clear, so that when life calls, we can respond from a position of power, rather than simply reacting. By being intentional, we deepen the quality of our decision-making and create the kind of life that is aligned with our deepest values and intentions.

How to Work on Developing Patience

Patience is a quality that would change the way we live our lives, reacting in a graceful manner to situations instead of making impulsive decisions and ultimately leading to less stress. Developing patience is something that we must consciously do and practice, but the rewards are priceless. This equips us with the custom of developing a patience and respond to situations skilfully which further acts as our strength to mobile through tougher times. A variety of practices exist to help cultivate patience—breathing practices, conscious pauses, and time-based practices like the "24-hour rule."

Breathe — Breathing exercises are one of the easiest and most impactful techniques you can use to develop patience. Feeling hurried or stressed or upset, we fraction our breath — manner out of breath, hurried, which exacerbates the urgency or impatience. Sighing, deep inhalation and exhalation, stretched breathing triggers the opposite response to what happens when we are anxious triggering relaxation mechanisms. Start by finding a calm environment, closing your eyes and deep breathing through your nose for a 4 count. Pause for a moment with the breath held, and slowly breathe out for a count of 6. Do this three to four cycles of breaths, feeling how your breath feels. Practicing this calms the mind and the feeling of serenity can make one approachable and take things patiently.

Box breathing is a technique that improves patience by taking a deep breath, holding it, exhaling, and holding again for 4 seconds each. This dynamic breathing will center your mind so you regain power over restlessness or impatience. The more you practice these exercises the more they literally train your mind to slow down, a skill which can be the most valuable in stressful or high-pressure situations.

Taking mindful pauses is another effective method to cultivate patience. Mindful pauses are about pausing and noticing what is going on in your mind and body prior to your reaction. If you find yourself in a situation that could trigger impatience, pause for a few seconds and observe what you are feeling. Take time to notice your own frustrations, stresses, or urgency and do your best to resist acting on this immediately. This little break can change your instinctual response to a careful reaction. When you notice your feelings nonjudgmentally, you develop a greater awareness of how impatience works its way into your mind and your body, making it easier to rein in these hormones.

Another way to develop patience is to practice based on time. The "24-hour rule" is one of the better-known time-based techniques. The 24-hour rule encourages you to challenge yourself to wait at least 1 day and 1 night before you make any big life decisions that happen mostly because you feel really strongly about something. For example, if you are feeling the need to go out and buy something know you are going to regret, making a purchase while angry or making a life decision that could have far-reaching consequences, then the 24-hour rule allows you time and distance to think. A lot of the time with a day between you and the urgency, you look at it in a different headspace. It keeps you from making an impulsive decision that you can end up regretting on a later date, it requires patience and being smart about how you act.

A second time-based practice is to create mini-waiting periods in the course of the day as an antidote to impatience. For instance, if you want to grab your phone, reply to a text, or get a task done, force yourself to pause for a few minutes before you act. Begin delaying these for a short period of time before gradually increasing this timeframe when you find yourself feeling more comfortable with waiting. These tiny delays stretch your waiting-accommodation and grow your patience, bit by bit, micro, by micro.

These techniques can be a way to slowly spin patience into your daily routine. It may take months, but with daily practice you will undoubtedly find yourself in fewer scrambles and be less reactive and better at being patient with delays or obstacles. A patient mind leads to less stress, better relationships, smarter decisions, and improvement in overall mental health. When you choose patience as a way of life, you can handle your daily battles with more strength because you have less fear to control you and more peace which leads to a higher quality of life.

Beating the Decision Fatigue

Decision fatigue is a term that describes the mental exhaustion we feel when we make too many decisions in one day. It tends to create bad decisions, spur of the moment planning, or even an entire shutdown of decision making. Given that every day consists of seemingly never-ending choices — from these small, mundane tasks to bigger, life-altering decisions — the burden of making decisions all day long can weigh us down. The first step toward escaping decision fatigue is spotting the signs deciding overload and replacing it with strategies that help us make decisions with clarity and purpose.

Identifying the signals of decision fatigue is the key to combating it. A sure sign is having a feeling of being overwhelmed or frustrated by even the smallest decisions. Options that may seem trivial or simple such as what to eat for dinner or what to wear can become overwhelming or heavy. Impulsivity: A sure sign of decision fatigue is that our impulsivity increases; we are low on mental energy, so we may hurry or make careless decisions to get them over with. It leads to bad decision making like buying things that are not important, focusing on things that are not that important, and saying yes to things without thinking it through. Then a third sign is procrastinating, which means we are so mentally drained by the choices we made prior, that we either want to put off making more decisions, and/or we are avoiding decisions that we have to make. The first step in combating decision fatigue is to identify these signs.

By spotting decision fatigue, we can start taking measures to reduce its effects. Well one way to remedy this issue is to cut the amount of decisions we have to make by creating routines. When we create rituals for things we do every day — what time do we get up in the morning, what do we eat for breakfast, or what time do we start or end work, we eliminate the need to make repetitive decisions about those activities. When we automate these decisions we have more mental space open for the important or complex decisions. Thinking ahead can eliminate some of that cognitive load — for instance, by planning each week's meals in advance, since choosing what to eat every day requires a lot of mental energy, and having a morning routine, as you wear the habit whether you really think about it or not — you wake up and you simply do your morning routine, you will just need to think about what you wear to do all this.

Alternatively, decisions can be prioritized by classifying them as high- or low-priority. Thoughtful deliberation is appropriate for high-priority decisions; low-priority decisions, rather than being overly complicated, should often be reduced to a simpler question, or, just decided by someone else. As an example, if a decision on the direction of a project is a top priority, the focus should be on that decision. That makes high-priority choices — such as what to wear — simpler when we have a set wardrobe or a capsule closet. It allows us to preserve our focus over time by dedicating our mental energy only to the highest-priority decisions and preventing needless mental fatigue on unimportant things.

Another trick is to set boundaries around decision-making times. So rather than trying to be decisive all day, block out time to make important decisions. It could be giving your mornings strictly towards the business, or maybe designating a specific evening to focus on planning in your personal life. Focus the decisions to be made on set periods when will be making them, this reduces the mental fatigue from constantly transitioning between making decision and other tasks. It keeps the day free from important decisions creeping in and contaminating the other paths of the day, giving us fresh mental energy to approach the hard stuff.

One of the MOST effective ways to overcome decision fatigue is to limit options. Whether choosing a restaurant, buying things, or selecting leisure activities, the availability of too many options can be stressful and reducing the options is key to avoid overwhelm. The process is easier if you establish some criteria for making your choice in advance or reduce your options to two or three. To illustrate, if you have too many options to decide what movie to watch, you can narrow it down by viewing preferences such as genre and it does not take a toll on your brain anymore. It ensures time is not wasted and mental energy is also preserved since you do not have to look through so many choices only to come up undecided.

Integrating short breaks and mental rests into the day is key to avoiding decision fatigue. A few minutes pause, a little walk or mindfulness can reset the mind which can regain before making another decision. A few moments of mental rest is enough to refocus and make better decisions after, Just like self-care, sleep is an important factor in establishing the mental fortitude to make good decisions: A rested mind is less vulnerable to decision fatigue.

Identifying the signs of decision fatigue, taking steps to avoid decision burnout, can help us cultivate a more balanced approach where decision-making preserves our mental fuel and improves our living experience. Daily choices can be minimized by creating routines, we can eliminate unimportant ones, set boundaries, limit choices, and finally rest well, all of it makes decision-making a sustainable process. In this way, we escape the spiral of decision fatigue and take each decision with clarity, confidence and intention so that we will have both more and better choices and take a more empowered and guided approach to life.

4

Staying Present to Make Informed Choices

It is an important practice which helps you to ground yourself in the here and now, which leads to inner peace, clarity and strength. It is all about focusing on the present so that you can deal with life's challenges with ease and mindfulness. This chapter covers how you can use techniques for grounding and centering practice, and it guides you on how to practice mindfulness in your everyday life.

Grounding is the awareness of connecting yourself to your body (feel your feet) and your surroundings (notice what you see and hear), A great approach is the "5-4-3-2-1" method to activate your senses and ground your mind. Start with five things you can see (such as a tree out the window or the texture of a table) Next, become aware of four things you can physically feel – the cloth of your clothes, or the texture of the ground you are sitting or standing on. Next, notice three things you hear, two things you smell, and one thing you taste. This exposure and engagement of your senses distracts you from wild thoughts, and brings you back to the moment, which you need desperately when things get intense.

Conscious breathing is another great tool for grounding. Digging into deep breath movement in and out calms the mind and body, bringing us into a state of rest and relaxation. One easy tip is called the "4-7-8" breathing – you breathe in for four counts, hold the breath for seven counts, and breathe out slowly for eight counts. Go through this cycle a couple of times until you can feel yourself relaxing and your mind being present in the moment.

Grounding exercises, like standing barefoot on the earth, going for a walk, or even holding a grounding object like the aforementioned smooth stone, are physical ways to ground oneself. Connection to earth or an object that can ground our energy assists in releasing discomfort and provides a degree of safety and centering.

Being mindful about your daily routine can help you be more present during the day. Even something as basic as having a cup of tea can become a grounding ritual if you do it with your full attention. Concentrate on the warmth of the cup in your palms, the smell of the tea and the experience of it hitting your lips. Through these moments of intentional presence, you train your mind to remain present.

In the same way, if you fill your day with wandering mindless thoughts, practicing presence in common day things — walking, cooking, doing dishes, can feel your body weight on the ground far even more rooted then you are already. While walking, notice how your footsteps land, the texture of ground under your feet, and any sounds you might hear. Be aware of the colors, sounds and smells of the ingredients and the cooking while you prepare your meal. Such practices turn mundane tasks into everyday opportunities to be present.

Grounding and being present are not just tools, they are practices to be sart for the long haul. Practicing these approaches consistently will give you the tools to face the struggles of life with poise. This way, you are creating the way to a feeling full life, where every moment is a chance to connect with yourself and the outside world again.

Please make sure to explain how: Collecting Data, Not Assumptions.

Fast-forward to today, where assumptions have a way of sneaking into our thinking, distorting our perspectives and our decisions. Assumptions are mental shortcuts–often informed only by incomplete information or biases–that lead us away from the truth. If you want to ensure that you are making good choices and engaging in constructive interactions, you need to deal in facts, not impressions. This chapter discusses why you should steer clear of assumptions, the merits of sticking with the facts and how mindfulness can improve clarity of view.

So going back to the idea of avoiding making assumptions, it takes a real effort to pause and ask ourselves 'Is that what is really going on here? Assumptions occur when we try to fill voids of ignorance without verification. The classic example is the idea that when a friend does not reply to a text message, we immediately think, `oh they are angry with me'. Nevertheless, in reality, it could be an entirely different situation; they may just have been busy, maybe they did not see the message. Then we can challenge them because they are generally based on partial data and look for clarity.

Diving into the facts refers to keeping within the real and provable elements of a scenario. It means questioning, looking for proof, and being open to new ideas. The important thing is to spare a minute or two to look take place, ask and confirm instead of assume. So if a co-worker seems aloof, instead of thinking they are mad, you can approach them and ask if every thing is okay. It helps mitigate miscommunication and thus makes way for trust and communication.

Mindfulness is a magical way to clear your lens of sight and avoid assumptions. Mindfulness allows you to see situations for what they are instead of reacting immediately. One mindfulness practice that can be helpful is the beginner's mind, which involves trying to approach every situation like it is the first time you are experiencing it. This certain mindset allows you to be curious and open-minded to notice things that you would normally miss.

Another mindfulness tool that could be helpful is observing. At the point when the occasion presents itself, this is a period to witness the complete occasion as it transpired without judgment. Focus on what you see, hear, and feel. And separate objective reality vs. subjective experience. As an example, if somebody speaks to you sharply, take their words and tonality instead of putting a story like "they don't like me". It helps you respond rather than react.

They can also help with cultivating a clear and calm mind. When you feel yourself about to assume, close your eyes and take three or four breaths. This very act provides room for contemplation, allowing you to gauge the situation with more perspective. You can also avoid impulsive judgments and stay focused on collecting accurate information by calming your nervous system.

All of this takes time and practice, but avoiding assumptions and dealing in facts is the key. It requires you to be with the moment, to not jump to conclusions, but to seek the understanding. They can strengthen your relationships, and lead you to better decisions over time. Prioritising facts allows you not just to view events clearly, but to develop an attitude of enquiry. This transition allows you to feel more confident, focused, and compassionate while doing life!

Intuition Vs Fear: How to Tell Them Apart

Maybe the hand that guides your will and holds your attention really is divine like these beliefs try to convince you; intuition and fear are powerful teachers and make strong illusions. Intuition is a profound, instinctual understanding that arises without conscious thought, and fear is a defensive reaction to a sense of imminent danger, shaped by past experiences or invisible threats. In order to make choices in keeping with who we really are, we need to differentiate between knowledge that is coming from our higher selves, and reactions that stem from fear. In this chapter we would find out what intuition was, what fears were, how to differentiate between the two, and golden tips and exercises to strengthen and have confidence in our intuition.

Intuition is a slow and clear voice — the one that arises when the mind is quiet, not overthinking. Its more of a gentle push or a part of your realisation that speaks to the heart not the brain. Fear, for example, is characterized by panic, urgency, and despair. Although fear is vital for signaling where we need to defend ourselves against genuine threats, it can also be misleading, particularly if it originates from different places – insecurity, history of trauma, or social conditioning.

Both intuition and fear can be differentiated from one another by observing the tensions in the body and the feelings they generate. Intuition always feels quite stable and grounded even when it is signalling a difficult decision. On the other hand, fear tends to be very chaotic and overwhelming, activating our fight or flight instinct. For example, if you are contemplating a new job offer, an intuition will whisper to you to go for it, and fear will yell to you how it will end up as a failure, and you will have to quit in no time.

An important part of comprehending these forces is locating the source of your emotions. Question yourself if your reaction is resulting due to present real truths or fictional situations. Intuition lives in the present, it guides you in the way of the real you. Fear, on the other hand, often pulls you into "what if" so it can instill needless reluctance or panic. Awareness takes practice and attention.

Reflective exercises are one way to reinforce the connection to intuition. Writing in a journal helps you clarify your thoughts and determine what your feelings really are. If you have to make a decision between two or more options, describe your first impressions, then see how they feel; calm and grounded (intuitive) or agitated and all over the place (fear). As you practice longer, you start to recognise your intuitive voice through patterns.

Meditation is a great tool for accessing your intuition. When we calm our minds and bring our awareness into the now, we make room for our intuition to emerge. One of the more simple examples of a meditation would be to sit in a quiet location, shut your eyes, and concentrate on taking deep breaths. We acknowledge that thoughts will arise, but approach them non-judgmentally as they pass like clouds in the sky. When you are in this still frame, you can better align with your true self.

Improving your ability to trust intuition Body-awareness exercises can also help. Often times your body will respond to intuitive signals long before your conscious mind even frames the thoughts. Tightness or lightness in your stomach, chest, or shoulders can tell you how you really feel, for example. Try to scan your body when you are making a choice, and you will start to notice these small signals.

Ultimately, trusting your intuition is acting on it in small intentional steps. Begin with lower-level choices, like where to eat or what to do, and see what happens. Notice how it feels to follow your intuition; what does that teach you? When you trust your intuition in this way, you are simply helping yourself be prepared when it comes to using it for big life decisions.

Distinguishing between intuition and fear allows you to interpret what decision resonates more deeply with you. When received meaning me having faith in them not to go wrong, it guides me through the struggles wherever their and my life may take us. Effective at times, fear inflicts a pulse of control over you until you wise up to its presence and give it conscious response. By owning this knowledge, you can move through your life with clarity, confidence, and the deep trust of your own knowing.

5

Managing Stress and Anxiety in Decisions

Stress, which is a natural reaction to the problems we face, can have a very big impact on our thoughts, feelings, and behaviour. Under pressure, our gut-level decision making works differently than we may consciously realize. Stress-filled decisions are the ones we make not when we are clear or intentional, but rather when we are rushed or blindsided with stress. In order to make decisions that are in our true best interest we need to understand how stress influences the way we make decisions and how it distorts our judgment.

A sense of urgency is one of the earliest signs of behavioral changes from stress that are affecting decision-making. When we are stressed, our fight-or-flight response kicks in, and our brains tend to favor immediate fixes rather than contemplation. Which may lead to snap judgments made without proper consideration of the ramifications. And an overwhelmed person might say yes to new projects or responsibilities just to avoid an argument, despite knowing that it will only contribute to their stress. It makes us more susceptible to weight options that will lead to instantaneous relief instead of long-term gain.

Yet another manifestation of bad decisions due to stress is reduced ability to focus or think. Stress affects cognitive functions, which means that we may struggle to pay attention to detail or to critically reflect on the information we are receiving. This usually leads to disregarding variables or misreading values. E.g. A person experiencing inner stress may misinterpret an email or blank out in a conversation.

Stress-induced decisions are also characterized by emotional reactivity. Under stress it is harder to separate feelings from facts, and many of those feelings are amplified. But the decisions we take when we are filled with emotion will always be reactionary, from a place of fear, anger, or frustration. A person might, for instance, fly off the handle in a meeting, or step out of a project entirely, not because that is the best thing to do, but because their emotions have outweighed their ability to rationalise what is the right course of action.

Stress can make people feel like they have a tunnel vision – it can tunnel our perspective. But when your mind is overwhelmed, it concentrates on what poses an immediate threat or difficulty, instead of what potentials are out there. This narrow perspective stifles creativity and adaptability, producing decisions based on what may be rational at the time but missing the big picture. As an example, if a leader is feeling pressure, they may cut costs by losing critical resources, only to find out down the road that those resources were vital to the success of the organization.

Stress distorts the judgment in ways that can really make a difference. When we have limited time and resources, we tend to look for quick, short-term fixes rather than long-term solutions. And that's because, when in stress mode, the brain is literally wired to solve the most immediate threat to survival and does not address longer term considerations. Furthermore, stress can also warp perceptions of risk and reward, resulting in risk aversion or risk seeking behaviour. An investor, under stress, may leave the market too early, forgo potential profits, or put money on a high-risk investment to make back all they lost soon.

Taking the decision is mostly done from stress, so it requires a conscious awareness of this process that it is guide by stress. If we pay attention to how we feel both physically and emotionally, we will be able to recognize those times when stress is triggered. And your feeling might be anxiety, panic attack, with symptoms of racing heart, breathlessness, or muscular tightness for physiological cue or signs of irritability, indecision, or overstimulated For emotional cue. It is time to stop and take stock when these things happen.

So you have to mitigate the effects of stress on decision-making by creating the space for reflection and grounding. Simple strategies, like deep breathing, writing in a journal, or going for a quick walk can help to reset a person mentally and physically. The break in the cycle between thought and action takes the mind from reactive to deliberate. The same goes for asking trusted friends, colleagues, or mentors for their perspective — weighing your options mindedly and with a pen in hand.

Recognizing the signs of stress-driven decisions and understanding both how stress distorts judgment will help us to mitigate its effects. Stress is inescapable but we do not have to act on it. By staying aware of the incentives that specific difficult circumstances have on our behaviour, and proactively developing strategies to sidestep these pitfalls, we can move through those situations with more clarity, so that our choices better align not just with what the moment demands of us, but what we really want to do. This opens up room for conscious decisions that benefit our mental health and are aligned with the future we desire for ourselves.

This article is a part of the series Fix Your Own Stress and Is Mindfulness Necessary for You? Type flexible methods of stress reduction.

Stress is a part of life, and it happens, but our response to it is a whole lot more telling when it comes to whether it affects our health or not. Stress occasionally motivates and gives energy to us, however ongoing or unaddressed stress impacts the health of mind and body. A solution to this is mindfulness, which reduces stress and builds a sense of peace in the present moment. By engaging in mindful practices such as meditation, deep breathing, or relaxation techniques, mindfulness helps them cope with stress and restore equilibrium.

One of the best techniques for relieving stress and an integral part of mindfulness — is meditation. Meditation is simply taking the time to pay attention and clearing your mind of racing thoughts. To begin a simple practice of meditation, find a quiet place and sit comfortably. Now close your eyes, relax and focus on the feeling of your breath going in and out. When thoughts come up — and they will — notice, without judgment, and bring your focus back to your breath. Practicing this for even a couple of minutes every day can help in reducing the stress as it calms the mind and creates clarity.

Deep breathing exercises are also a great way to relieve stress because they balance your nervous system, which inhibits some of the physical effects of stress. One popular method is called diaphragmatic (or belly) breathing. Try this: — Put one hand on your chest and one hand on your abdomen, now take a deep nose inhale, the hand on your abdomen should rise while the hand on your chest should stay still Now, open your mouth and exhale slowly, allowing your stomach to come down. This points out the annoying reaction of the physique, the battle-or-flight mode set up during tension, by activating the leisure reaction of the physique.

Progressive muscle relaxation is another mindfulness-based method that helped reduce physical tension commonly related to stress. This method consists of a progressive tightening and loosening of different muscle groups in the body. First, tense the muscles in the toes for a few seconds and release them while concentrating on the sensation of relaxation. Try systematically moving through your body — toes to legs to tummy to arms to shoulders to face. Not only does this help alleviate tension in the body, but in tandem with this practice, it also helps develop awareness of the connection between mind and body.

Stress management through mindfulness is not just about doing some techniques, its about creating a mental state which brings you back to the present moment. Stress takes the mind on a journey — either into the future where the body is anxious about what may come, or into the past where the search for solutions lies. Mindfulness interrupts this cycle by anchoring you in the present. For instance, when you feel a build-up of tension, stop and do a mini body scan. Notice your body from the head down, gently observing the feelings in your body, but not changing them. And this practice really encourages you to accept what is, and that can be extremely peaceful.

To provide a long-lasting solution to stress, incorporate mindfulness in your daily activities as it is a factor one should keep in mind. Any activity done daily — walking, eating or even washing dishes — can turn into mindfulness practice. Focus on the cadence of your walk and the texture of the ground you are walking on. When you eat, experience the flavors, textures, and smells of what you are eating using all of your senses. These practices keep stress levels low and add wealth and presence to day-to-day living.

Mindfulness changes your relation to stress, and that is why it is so powerful. Mindfulness invites you to meet stressful situations with curiosity and openness rather than resisting or fearing them. Recognizing your stress (nonjudgmentally) allows yourself to respond to challenges more clearly and more resiliently. With practice, mindfulness is a tool you can use to move through the hard things in life with ease, approaching stress with serenity and self-assurance.

By integrating meditation, deep breathing, and relaxation practices into your regular routine, you will build a solid foundation for stress management. When coupled with an intention to stay present and aware, both of these methods help mitigate the short term effects of stress while also creating a greater sense of balance and harmony over time. Mindfulness gives the empowering seat of control to you, doing life with ease even when life is life-ing.

Handling the Uncertainty and Anxiety

Uncertainty is a naturally occurring part of life. Be it a decision that is pending, a career transition, or simply an unclear future, the unknown often comes with discomfort and anxiety. Coping with uncertainty is an act of mindfulness — not falling into the trap of the unknown but not ignoring it either. However, with a few mindful habits and some concrete tactics, you can mitigate anxiety and see through the haze ahead of making these high-stakes decisions.

To approach uncertainty mindfully, start by recognizing that uncertainty is neither good nor bad; it just is. A lot of fear of the unknown often comes from wanting to control an anxiety that we really have no control over. Mindfulness allows us to tolerate this discomfort, to observe how we feel, and how our mind responds without being totally absorbed by them. So if you were unsure about a big decision like moving or going somewhere else for work, mindfulness would say focus on the moment and not try to get lost in "what if" situations. By realizing a large part of the anxiety around the unknown is due to thinking about the future, you can focus on what you can actually control.

Grounding Fit in the Present One practice with uncertainty is to ground us in the potential to be out of the present. As you feel the fear about the unknown start to spiral in your mind, stop and breathe slowly, a few deep breaths. Turn your awareness to your physical body and your environment — the ground beneath your feet, the air against your skin, or the movement of your breath. To take deep breaths so we can be mindful creates a space between you and those feelings where we can respond instead of react.

One of the most important skills needed to cope with uncertainty is learning to accept. Acceptance is not accepting that you cannot control anything but knowing what you can control and giving up the rest. If you are waiting to hear back from a job interview, concentrate on what you can control, like reading for future questions you might get asked again or looking for other roles. That helps re-direct your energy from fretting over the results to doing something positive instead.

Given the mental stress that high-stakes choices often trigger, practical strategies can help you cope with the high-pressure situations to make better decisions with less anxiety. A great way to do this is by splitting the steps to make a decision. If you are trying to determine if you should take on a new business venture, start by digging up information pertaining to it, such as financial forecasts or market research. Then, discuss your situation with trusted mentors or colleagues. You actually work your way through each part of the decision and slowly the sense of being overwhelmed starts to dissipate and you become clearer.

Another technique is when you being doubt, you have to show self-compassion. Self-criticism is common when anxiety arises, thoughts like "Oh no, what if I mess this up?" or "I can't do this." Change these thoughts by treating yourself like a friend. Tell yourself that not knowing what to do is a part of evolution and that even choosing wrong does not mean you are worthless. By practicing self-compassion, you keep your insides cushy, meaning that your ability to make decisions becomes more adaptive.

Visualization is one of those tools for easing anxiety in high-stakes decisions. Now picture that best possible outcome of your decision and how your heart would feel to achieve it. Then, take an example of the steps you would take to achieve that. That practice of stillness not only fosters peace of mind but also a sense of agency — it will serve as a reminder that you are in command and are capable of weathering storms.

Lastly adapt a mindset that sees uncertainty as an opportunity rather than a risk. What if the unknown spaces are where we grow and create and discover? This mental re-framing takes the emphasis off fear and places it instead on curiosity and this allows you the freedom to explore the possible instead of being stifled by fear.

Learning to cope with uncertainty and anxiety is a process, it takes time, and practice. But if you are able to practice eyes wide open uncertainty, feel rooted where are you are now, and utilize tried and true methods to lower anxiety, you will be able to traverse through the roughest waters quietly and deliberately. As time goes, you will see uncertainty as a gateway to new possibilities and personal development, and no longer a source of anxiety.

6
Building Confidence in Your Choices

A big part of being able to living comfortably in your own skin is trusting your decision-making process, That self-doubt can get in the way of good decision making and even lead to hesitation, second-guessing or paralysis when it comes to a choice. Self-awareness, supported by a strong sense of self-trust, is the foundational principle of the skill of building trust in your decisions. Combining mindfulness with intentional reflection on previous experiences is an effective way to bolster this trust and face the choices of life with greater certainty.

It starts with anchoring yourself in the here and now. When you are constantly worrying about the future, and fearing that you will make the wrong decision, or when you are regretting the past and feeling that everything could have been different if something else was done. Practising mindfulness allows you to distance yourself from this noise in the mind and choose decisions with clarity instead of decisions based on anxiety. When you become more present, you connect with your intuition and your values, the real basis of good decisions.

Mindfulness in decision making is slowing down to allow pause before we move forward. Tune into your mind and body and notice your thoughts and feelings with compassion, as much as you can, when you have a choice. And so as you're about to delete the back-end, ask yourselves: What is motivating this decision? Is this consistent with my value system and long range goals or brought on by peer pressure or transitory feelings? By questioning, you are able see what is important to you and gradually you start to trust your ability to do a good job in deciding.

Forgiveness also breeds self-trust when you accept lack of perfection. Not every decision leads to perfection and perfection causes needless self-loathing. Mindfulness allows you to accept that uncertainty exists and that every decision, even the ones that lead you to difficulties, has its lessons. If you can drop the anchor of needing to know with 100% certainty, you can start to move with awe and experience (confidence and resilience!).

Another key practice to help get trust in your decision making is to reflect on past choices. That history is written with your choices, right — choices that worked out, choices that did not, but all of them leading you down a path and giving you a chance to learn along the way. Revisit these moments, not by judging yourself, but by exploring. Think about decisions you made in the past that ended up being right and try to pinpoint the traits that helped them be successful—was it a clear allocation of role, thoroughly mapped out strategy, or calculated risk?

Also, reflect on decisions that were wrong leads to the outcome not happened. Do not see these choices as failures but instead as opportunities to learn. What insights did you gain? How do they get you ready for the challenges ahead? Looking at the decisions you made as a skill that matured and perhaps underwent iterations from experience to experience. Recognizing your growth gives you trust in yourself in what you can tackle next.

One way to incorporate this reflective practice is through journaling. Document important choices you have received the opportunity to make and think through why you made them. What emotions were present? Q: Did any external pressures influence the process? How did the eventual outcome compare to what you were hoping to achieve? Journaling can help you to identify clogs in your decision-making process, strengths, and maybe some decision-making problems. Doing this regularly also helps you build trust in yourself that you can make intentional decisions.

Staying true to yourself means share to trust about your decision-making process. Your perspective is your own no one has been through what you have where you are and who you are so unique, with your values and insights from all the experiences of life to draw on. C Comparison like B Comparison, can put you into a state of self-doubt and can take away your confidence in your choices. Mindfulness helps you appreciate your point of view and trust that you know what you need better than anyone else. Being yourself provides a clear roadmap for decision-making that can be in line with your true essence.

In essence, extracting trust in your decision-making process takes practice, patience, and grace. Whatever you do, right or wrong or from where you go, you will learn and grow with every single choice you make. Having a constantly remind you that you can trust yourself in every situation by creating decisions mindfully but also by being reflective about your experiences. It allows you to step into the future with the confidence that, no matter what lies ahead, you have the ability and fortitude to deal with it all.

Conquering Second Thoughts and Impostor Syndrome

The mind can hold onto events from the past that no longer serve you in the form of regret, that ultimately lead to self-doubt. The eerie what if thoughts — what if I could have done something else, what if I responded faster — builds a negative reflection loop that kills your confidence and resilience. To free yourself of, these feelings you should not forget the past but rather reframe the way you see things and build up compassion for yourself to be able to move forward without regret and full of strength and clarity.

Understanding that many a regret comes from wanting to change things that cannot be changed is where the letting go of "what if" thoughts begins. A decision made at a different moment in time represents the knowledge, feelings, and context of that era of your life. Looking back on those times, with the benefit of hindsight, can make things seem like they could have turned out differently. The only way to free ourselves from this cycle is to recognize and accept the truth that we can not change the past but learn from it.

Mindfulness is a beautiful way to be with regret, by anchoring yourself in the present moment. So when the thoughts of "what if" come in, just remember take a breath and bring your attention back to the present moment. Recognize your emotions — sadness, frustration, or disappointment and understand these feelings are natural, but not lasting. By allowing the choices of the past to be part of your unique journey you begin to shift your attention away from what is done to what can still be done.

Regret also comes fueled by self-doubt, as you beat the internal drum with negative self-talk and question your ability. It is important to practice self-compassion to help overcome this phenomenon, which means treating yourself the way you would treat your best friend. Realize that most decisions come from a place of effort and intention rather than criticism you can give yourself for making mistakes. You might have chosen based on little information, or on a wish, even if the aim is not what you wished. Knowing this creates compassion for yourself, a softening of the severe nature of self-criticism.

Part of exercising self-compassion is reframing the story of your regrets. The next time you perceive a choice as a mistake, instead see it as an experience that deepened your knowledge of life. A career track that went awry may have led you to develop resilience, connect with great people, or know what you want to do. Each and every action, even when it comes with annoyances, is a piece of the power of you. When you learn lessons you turn your regret into your power.

Despite what the self-doubt feels like, doing practices to strengthen your belief in yourself will build resilience against it. Think back to times in the past when you have met challenges, no matter how small. Maybe you went with the flow of a surprise development, managed a disagreement, or picked up a technique you did not initially want to embrace. They are living proof of your ability to endure and of the choices you made that created a positive outcome. Reflecting back on these successes is a reminder that the voice of self-doubt is short-lived and that you possess the skills to carry forward.

A more-disciplined way to put some closure on regret and self-doubt, however, is to create a forward-moving intent. Choose one small, doable opportunity that you can create or one piece of what feels broken that you can heal. If for example, you realized that you would have liked to have worked in some particular profession, you might take an online course in that field, reach out to people in that profession, or volunteer. Action combats the feeling of powerlessness, making the choice to move forward a powerful demonstration of agency and purpose — a small act of defiance against believing the future must look like the past.

It also comes from surrounding yourself with those that believe in you, who support your path toward your best self, and who accept you as you are. Talk to a friend, family member, or mentor about your feelings of regret or doubt. By hearing their perspective can give you a new outlook, and a reminder that you are not the only one going through it. Sometimes just talking about your problems, breaks through and gives the perspective needed — thank you.

Dealing with regret and lack of confidence is a lifelong process of mindfulness and intention. It takes time and the ability to accept your mistakes are part of the human experience. When you let go of the "what if" thoughts and give yourself self-compassion, you can break the chains of regret and regain your power. Every moment is a new opportunity to rewrite your story, not to erase your history, but to evolve beyond it, embracing the lessons and strength within you. Believe that you can and will grow and keep taking those steps, no matter how small, in the confidence that you are discovering your way to YOU!

Affirming Positive Outcomes

A great way to live is to have good vision. Every decision we make, small or large, creates our path – and asserting their goodness can move the mind from doubt to confidence. We make room for possibility and self-reliance that propels our growth and success by using gratitude for the choices of the past and visualization of what works.

To be grateful for past decisions, it starts with acknowledging the benefit that those decisions have given you in your life. Even dish decisions which might not have pan out the way we hoped tend to teach us hidden lessons or create unexpected opportunities. Finding gratitude in these moments reframes the story of your journey and focuses on the opportunities, the growth, the everything that happened because of your choice to pursue entrepreneurship.

Identify the choices you can take pride in, however simple they may be. Maybe you took a job that was more fulfilling, or you broke up with someone who was doing you no good, or you practiced patience for a hobby that has become an important part of life. When you acknowledge these moments you are reinforcing that you are the type of person who can make choices that lead to good things.

It can even help you see the good in decisions that at one point seemed to be the wrong decision. Reflect on how those instances instilled resilience within you, prioritization, or opened up new dimensions of seeing things. For example, an intimidating career switch at the time could have pointed you toward what you were meant to do. When you shift from regret to gratitude by seeing the lessons built into these experiences, you remove the regret from the equation.

To regularly nurture this appreciation, try maintaining a gratitude journal focused on decisions. Everyday take one decision you made previously which influences your life to set to grow and write it down. Making decisions that stand on the foundation of reflection do make history and wireless you more too yourself on a journey of future decisions.

Another method of affirming positive possibilities is visualizing successful outcomes. The mind is an extremely powerful instrument, and by imagining success, you prepare yourself and are more likely to act with confidence and purpose. This is where visualization plays a role, as it will help you with not only thoughts in your mind, but also with imitating initial actions directed towards your goal, which creates a blueprint of your objective in your head.

Find a quiet place where you can focus to begin practicing visualization. Imagine a time where you made decisions which lead to success — go ahead and close your eyes. Visualize all the details: what the surroundings look like, how you feel, and how others react to you and relate to you. So if you have a big presentation coming up, imagine yourself confidently making the presentation, the audience being engaged, and it going well. The more sensory-immersive your visualization is, the more you confirm your confidence in your success.

Another good exercise to visualize is to imagine watching a movie of your successful desired result. Visualise yourself achieving that goal in as much detail as possible, moving towards it, overcoming obstacles, and getting to the end result; almost as if you were watching a film of it in your mind. Visualizing this thought-movie over and over spreads conviction and therefore, serves as a reminder of your dedication to the process.

You can combine visualization with affirmations to make the visualization more effective. Positive affirmations, are statements that support the belief you have in yourself and the positive things you want to achieve. For example, repeat to yourself, "I can make decisions that bring about success," or "Every decision I make, puts me one step closer to my goal." Daily reciting these affirmations establishes a mindset of positivity and self-confidence.

Practicing gratitude and visualisation sets a mindset that celebrates your past decisions and hopes for your future. It allows you to face difficulties with tenacity and see new paths with excitement. It is not disregarding all the pain, but it is recognizing that you have the ability to fight through it and still do what you set out to do. Your confidence in decision-making gradually built on this practice allows you to craft a life based on your truest desires.

7

Mindful Decision-Making in Relationships

Our relationships are one of the biggest parts of our lives and they determine how we see ourselves and the meaning we give to the world. They also shape the decisions we make, often attracting or pushing us in invisible or obvious directions. These dynamics can often play out in our unconscious minds as we make decisions, and we must navigate them mindfully with a dedication to open lines of communication and very clear boundaries.

Decisions impact by Relationships in manner that usually goes unnoticed. The wants, desires, opinions, perceptions, and expectations of the people closest to us—partners, family, friends, or coworkers—can influence what we do (either on course with our own purpose or success or contrary to it, too). For example, because a parent wants their child to become a doctor, their child may eventually turn out to be one, even if they know medicine is not their passion. Likewise, the fear of letting your partner or friend down will make you make decisions more to get out of the relationship with them.

A first step to undermining these influences is to be aware of them. It might help to consider if a decision, which you feel you are making, is entirely yours or if it is one that was born from the wishes of others, and/or the expectations of others. Things like "Is this decision made because it aligns with who I am and what I want for my life, or because I am scared of the way someone else will respond? By practicing mindfulness, you can separate external expectations from internal desires, enabling you to make decisions that align with your true self.

Whether or not we see eye to eye with a person, mindful communication has a big part to play. Communication — Approach communication with a clear and open mindset where the goal is understanding vs frequency associated with it, this will help eliminate misunderstandings which is usually the basis of many arguments in a relationship. Similarly when you want to communicate or express something or make a decision, mindfulness promotes doing so with more intention and awareness, using a language that best expresses how you feel but at the same time being accommodating towards the other party as well. Instead of saying, "you never support my ideas," write what you feel using "I feel… when…" statements like "I feel unsupported when you don't consider my ideas."

Mindful communication also rests on the idea that one listens fully. A lot of the time, the conversations within relationships are just a war about who can get their point across better, without either side listening. Active listening allows you to immerse yourself fully into what the other is saying and feeling while allowing the other to feel understood and appreciated. This could look like maintaining eye contact, nodding or indicating that you are listening, and not interrupting someone when they are speaking. Not only does mindful listening improve comprehension — it also builds connection and trust.

Setting boundaries, adhering to them too however is equally necessary for a wholesome relationship dynamic. Boundaries are the walls we put up to keep ourselves emotionally healthy, and they help determine how we allow others to treat us. Mindfulness empowers you to recognize when others are testing your limits, pushing your boundaries, or may need to be put in place again with new limits. Say a friend regularly calls during your work hours; mindfulness gives you the recognition that it is a source of stress, and allows you to express a boundary: "I enjoy talking to you, however, I need to work during the day. Can we talk in the evening instead?"

Equally as important is respecting other people and their boundaries. Mindfulness helps you respond with acceptance instead of a defensive reaction when someone expresses a need or boundary. For instance, when a partner requests some time away to pursue personal passion projects, rather than seeing this as a sign of rejection, being mindful allows you to see this as an act of self-care that enhances the relationship.

Part of mindfully practicing relating is knowing all relationships can not be controlled. Although you can do your best to promote understanding and respect, it helps to remember that people come with their own story, history and responses. This mindfulness helps you to soften towards these differences instead of judging both of you, so that the two of you can feel safe to express, say, one to another.

With mindfulness you can be more aware of yourself, communicate more deliberate and respect boundaries when it comes to relationships. This makes the behavior more reinforcing toward health-positive behavior and less likely for you to feel outside pressure making a decision that is not aligned with your values and priorities. At the end of the day, mindful relationships give you the ability to navigate the dynamic where the well pillar of yourself interacts with all others; so these are built on pillars of mutual respect, understanding and authenticity.

Handling Conflict Mindfully

Human relationships are key to the fabric of our world, and with relationships — comes conflict. In both private and professional spheres, differences of opinion arise from conflicting perspectives, requirements, or expectations. Even though we may feel uncomfortable during conflict, it is a sign that we are alive, that we are moving and we get an opportunity to understand our differences and to bond in a better way. Mindful conflict management means not reacting but being empathetic and listening to each other, which lays the groundwork for resolving issues while still being respectful to each other.

The first step in dealing with conflict mindfully is to control your initial responses to conflict. And that button you are about to be pushed, which will bring out in you a flood of emotional responses – anger, frustration, hostility, defensiveness. These reactions can amplify tensions and create more difficulty in resolving them. One of the things you will learn from mindfulness practice is to sit with an urge to react, creating space to process a situation rationally instead of emotionally. The next moment you sense the tide of a reactive impulse, breathe and reconnect with the here and now. That moment of pause gives you space to feel your feelings and respond thoughtfully instead of reactively.

A great technique for not blowing your top is the habit of separating from judgment. Most of the time though, at the height of our emotions, anything said or done is taken as a personal affront. Mindfulness holds that the act, and the person who performed it, are not one in the same, and that the behavior must take priority over the person to be blamed. Show some empathy—for instance, instead of flaring up defensively because a coworker has been curt, ask yourself if their tone is due to stress or other elements of their life. Now, instead of confrontation, this perspective leaves room for fruitful dialogue.

Empathy: Practicing empathy is the first step to mindful conflict resolution. Short version: Empathy means putting yourself in the other persons shoes and trying to see their feelings and motivations. And even when we disagree, it helps us to feel connected, and respected. Start off by validating that the experience of the other person is real and true, even though it may be different to yours. For example, during a confrontation with a friend, you could say: "I understand that you have been very upset about this case, and I want to know more about what you feel.

Mindful Communication Active listening is also very important for mindful conflict resolution. Often in heated moments, you aren't listening to the other person at all — you're just busy preparing your argument. This requires you to truly listen to what they are saying, as well as their feelings and needs. This entails eliminating distractions, maintaining eye contact, and nodding or providing verbal affirmations to indicate that you are paying attention. If there is something not clear, ask for clarification — something like, what do you mean (by that)? This either prevents misinterpretations or informs them that you value their viewpoint.

When you listen, also try to reflect it back to them, so both of you understand what was heard. For instance, you could say, "You sound like you are hurting; you felt like you were excluded from the decision. Is that right?" Reflective listening shows the person that you value the feelings they are expressing, and that you are trying to comprehend their perspective.

Unlike empathy and active listening, which is concerned with the other, mindful conflict resolution also consists of authentic expression of your own needs and feelings. When you express yourself with clarity and calm, you minimize the risk of being misunderstood and move the conversation in the direction of resolution. Expressing your views without blaming using "I" statements So instead of saying, "You never listen to me" reframe it to "I feel unheard when my ideas are not acknowledged in our discussions." It reframes blame into your experience, provoking conversation, rather than defense.

Finding common ground is also an part of conflict resolution. While conflict drives a wedge between two sides, if you highlight common goals or values, you redirect the dialogue. In a conflict at work over project priorities, you might say, so run de-escalation like:We both want this project to succeed. How can we coordinate to achieve the optimal outcome? It is this method which nurtures partnership and shared purpose.

Finally, do not expect every disagreement to be resolved at once or in ideal conditions. Mindfulness helps you accept this as a fact of life with grace and realize that the point is not to agree on everything, but to treat each other with respect and understanding. Some of the time, the best answer is concurring to return to the conversation later or recognizing that you can differ and still get along.

Handling conflict mindfully: You focus on the present moment and cultivate non-reactive behaviours, practicing empathy and listening actively so that you can turn the moment of conflict into a moment of meaning and connection. Resolving conflicts mindfully does not only settle disputes but also fortifies the connection, establishing a bond of trust and respect able to withstand future storms.

Making Collaborative Choices

At its core, collaboration is arguably the foundation of healthy relationships and productive teamwork. Personal or professional, in all sorts of collaboration the best choice is to keep your own needs balanced with those of the ones you are working with, doing so requires a level of respect and awareness understanding from both sides. In the presence of mindfulness and intentionality, collaboration changes decision-making from a solo performance that destroys relationships and leads to mediocre results, to shared labor that binds relationships and leads to higher quality outcomes for all actors in the system.

Maximizing your needs with other people necessitates clear goals and priorities around your own values. Before hopping into an environment of collaboration reflect on what you value the most when it comes to the choice that you are facing. Whether this is a joint family decision, group project, or business partnership — knowing your objective and your boundaries is key to working in harmony. Collaboration also needs a certain willingness to consider the ideas and interests of others. Understand that you may not be totally on the same wave length as far as priorities go.

Translate this into a curious and flexible frame of mind. Come to conversations with an open mind and be able to hear the conversation and explore options rather than holding onto a position. As an example, if deciding on a family vacation, you may prefer relaxation, but another family member may prefer adventure. Instead of framing it as a competing interest conversation, treat it as an opportunity to collaborate on designing a solution that embodies some of both preferences.

It also requires clear communication, which is also essential for effective collaboration. Stating your needs directly opens up people to understand your side, and in turn, listening to them can assure that they feel heard as well. Make sure to use the 1st person, also known as I statements, to communicate and not put blame or judgment. So instead of saying, "You always dismiss my ideas," say, "I feel dismissed when my ideas are not included. This is oriented much more towards collaboration than confrontation.

You want to engage in exercises that encourage deeper connection and empathy to foster respect and understanding for one another. Among them is called perspective-taking. In a conversation, consciously put yourself in the other person's shoes and try to envision how the situation may appear to them. Think about questions such as, "What could they be going through? What are the challenges or priorities influencing their view? With this mental framework, we go into a conversation with compassion which reduces miscommunication and allows more good faith.

A second great exercise would be working together to solve a problem. Instead of pitting one interest against another, make a decision as a challenge to overcome. Start with a Definition of the Problem and Let Everyone Have a Say. As an illustration, in a work context, if team members are arguing over what resources should be allocated, begin by saying something like, "What are the key objectives of this project, and how can we leverage our resources collectively to accomplish this? It allows the group to come up with creative solutions that can be mutually beneficial to meet different needs given that they are targeted on common goals.

Active listening — A basic practice of listening to understand not to respond This practice can change the course of any conversation and foster collaboration. Make a habit of being fully present with what they are saying and feeling during your conversations. Do not give in to your temptation to interrupt or plan your answer when he/she is talking. Rather, mirror what you heard as a way to verify understanding. For example, you could say: It sounds like you are worried about how this choice will impact our timeline. Is that right?" This helps to avoid miscommunication and also shows that you care about their opinion.

Adopting compromise offers another way of reinforcing mutual respect. In collaboration, there will often need to be compromise: sadly, no-one gets everything they want, but there needs to be common ground where all the core needs are being met. This doesn't look like compromising, but rather developing solutions that recognize how everyone contributes and what their priorities are. For instance, if two groups in a community planning meeting value green spaces and infrastructure respectively, a trade-off could be appropriately designed by combining the two in one plan.

Finally, choosing to work together takes time and requires us to think long-term. Some decisions will not be solved in one conversation and some compromises will also take time to execute. Keeping the addendum respectful and understanding will create an atmosphere of trust to allow for deeper and more productive collaborations in the future.

Collaboration is a fluid dance, one that requires vulnerability, honesty, and adaptability. You can make the balancing of your needs with those of others into a collaborative process in which mutual respect thrives and the outcomes are meaningful for all involved. Collaboration is not about the need to agree — if we all agreed, we would never co-create anything — but rather something even deeper that happens as we do: finding the solutions we need to honor each contribution and weave a fabric of trust and consecutiveness.

8
Applying Mindful Choices to Major Life Decisions

This is one of the biggest decisions we take, as career and finance are some of the key elements that will drive the direction of our life. Such options can be invigorating, naturally they can also lead to ambiguity and anxiety. Weaving mindfulness into the decision-making process enables you to address life changes relating to your career and finances with clarity, intention, and resilience, ensuring your decisions are working in your interest with respect to your values and long-term vision.

Mindfulness is the first step of self-awareness, which is an important component when assessing career paths, or financial goals. Career decisions can often involve more than just money, such as job satisfaction, financial security, and growth potential. Financial affairs too will involve choices, short-term versus long-term. In the midst of these complexities, mindfulness can provide you an opportunity to step back, reflect on what is truly important, and take only the actions that align to your vision.

The first step to a mindful approach to career decisions, is to ask yourself why. If your ideal career is already a reality or may soon be, think about what is most aligned with your values. Do you want more creativity, stability or impact potential? When you know what matters to you, external influence can be stripped away and you can make decisions based on what you need versus what you think you need. So, if you have a new job on the table that pays considerably more money and requires a lot of travel, being mindful will help you assess what the lost time with family, or the lost sense of work-life balance is really worth.

Mindful career navigation also means that you are able to identify any fears or limiting beliefs that might drive how you navigate your career. Decisions that come from avoidance rather than growth are those affected by fear—fear of failure, fear of the unfamiliar, or even just fear of your own abilities. Mindfulness invites you to watch these fears without allowing them to drive the bus. Therefore, when you are staring at a potential career change, take a moment and encourage yourself to consider not the risks alone, but also the possibilities and development that it may entail. Such a balance of perspectives creates a sense of empowerment and lessens the paralysis that fear creates.

Approaching financial decisions in a mindful way is a more optimal strategy, just like career decisions. Because money is like a wishful, emotional being that many apply subjectivity onto and attempt to imbue it with purpose in life (the hope for security, freedom, fear, etc.). In financial decision making or planning, mindfulness allows you to differentiate yourself from your emotional impulses. For instance, if you are about to make a significant purchase, take a moment to ask yourself whether that purchase is part of your long-term financial plan or merely a spontaneous emotional craving. That brief moment creates room in our mind to choose wisely.

Mindful financial planning starts with knowing what you to accomplish with your finances. If you are saving for a home, paying off debt, or saving for an emergency, mindfulness allows you to keep your eyes on the prize and not get distracted from what really matters to you. It helps to determine if what you are spending or saving for is what you want to be doing, so it is a good idea to review your financial priorities on a consistent basis. Rather than being concerned as to how everyone strives for the untold riches of riches and splendor, Mindfulness forces you to concentrate on those things that bring you real fulfillment and comfort.

In terms of money, just as mindfulness can make a huge difference when it involves budgeting. Budgeting takes an understanding of what types of spending you typically engage in, as well as the discipline to make changes when they make sense. Tracking expenses will open your eyes and help you take a closer look at patterns that support or work against your goals. For instance, timely and frequent impulse purchases may motivate a more deliberate approach to spending, such as reserving time to consider if each expense is up to your standards.

Mindfulness helps you manage uncertainty with perspective and patience when you are investing or planning for retirement. Financial planning, on the other hand, is invariably rife with times of doubt or fear because markets move. It helps you avoid knee jerk reactions to short-term fluctuations and stay focused on the bigger picture. Being aware of what is happening currently can help a business owner to make financial decisions based on strategy, not emotion.

Gratitude practice is also a mindful habit that works wonders on your money making and career. Gratitude pulls you from thinking in scarcity to abundance, teaching you that you can value what you have right now, while at the same time chase your goals in the future. For instance, being grateful for a steady paycheck or the knowledge you have acquired throughout your working life allow you to feel a sense of satisfaction despite your continued quest for greater heights.

It is not going to be a quick process from all your choices into how you navigate your career and your finances — and you need to treat yourself with kindness and patience to see this through. Temporary failure might also be the order of the day, but those are opportunities to be wiser, and wiser decisions will lead to better outcomes. In doing so, you can be centered and confident in making the larger and more pivotal decisions in life with all of the clarity. With mindfulness, career and money ceases to be a source of stress — instead they become a means of alignment and fulfillment, allowing you to create the life you truly desire.

Intentional Decisions in Health and Wellness

While health and well-being are an essential part of a good life, the ability to choose wisely in these realms among the noise of contradictory claims, societal expectations and busy lives is difficult. Mindfulness offers a route to greater clarity, allowing you to approach health-related decisions with the benefit of peacefulness, intention and insight in line with your values. With awareness and intention, you can make decisions that really align with your physical, mental, and emotional health.

The starting point for mindful health decision-making is by paying attention to your body and its diverse cues. Humanity has a reactive approach towards health where people think of it when problems arise. Mindfulness is the opposite, it teaches you to listen and connect with your body to notice when something is off before it becomes a problem. For example, noticing subtle signs of fatigue, stress, or discomfort can lead you to make timely choices like changing your diet, getting proper rest, or visiting a professional.

Making clear health-related decisions is also about shutting out the noise from outside influences. With ads pushing newest fitness craze to well-meaning friends and family sharing advice, the information overload can make it hard to figure out what will work for you. Mindfulness allows you to sift through this information by only concentrating on input that speaks to your goals and situation. Take a moment to consider a new exercise routine or change in diet and ask yourself if it suits your needs, your ability, and your lifestyle. This deliberate assessment ensures knee-jerk reactions to external forces of nature or short-lived fads do not compel one to make a decision.

Figuring out our emotions is essential to mindful choice of health. Eating, exercising, and self-care-related behaviors are often motivated by emotions and may not support longer-term well-being. Stress or boredom could activate overeating, while inadequacy could trigger extreme dieting or overexercising. Mindfulness helps you notice these emotional triggers while refraining from judgment, leaving room to respond instead of react. Rather than stressing out and consuming comfort food, you might opt for meditation, breathwork, or a peaceful stroll to solve the source of your stress.

Realistic and Compassionate Goals: A Mindful Dimension of Health Decision-Making Lack of patience can result in setbacks and progress stagnation through frustration, burnout, or self-criticism. Mindfulness promotes self-compassion in your health journey, knowing that you will not reach your goals in one day, and that setbacks are a natural part of the process. Mindfulness, for instance, helps you forget about guilt, if you skip a workout or eat junk food, because it reinforces that it is important to recenter your attention at the bigger picture, not sporadic misses.

If you have major health decisions to make: Picking a treatment plan or a lifestyle change, mindfulness can help you frame your decisions in an easier-to-manage way. Follow through with the appropriate information from trusted sources and, when necessary, professionals. Next, find a sacred space in which you can meditate on the decision: note the thoughts going through your mind, the feelings in your heart, and the body sensations. This practice helps you distinguish between fear or anxiety and true intuition, resulting in you being directed towards the decisions that align with you.

Mindfulness, too, is about small, sustainable behaviors — the kind that last and ultimately lead to long lasting wellness. Sweeping initiatives — like going on a crash eating regimen or signing up for a strenuous health mission — might work for a while, however are generally difficult to stick to. Rather, prioritize the simple, intentional habits that you can easily incorporate into your daily routine. Little wins · Ten minutes each morning to stretch · Snacking on fruit instead of sugar · Going to bed at a fixed time each night for goodness sake · These all seem like such tiny, petty wins in the moment, yet the cumulative effect can be monumental.

Highlighting gratitude on your health journey develops a positive outlook and fortifies your motivation. Gratitude changes the comparison from what you think you are missing to what you possess. When you appreciate your body for what it can do right now–walking, breathing, existing–you foster a gentler sense of respect, and that leads you to choose more nourishing options. When we show gratitude for small wins (taking the time to drink a glass of water or stay active for 5 minutes), we reinforce the feeling in our minds that something is progressing, that we are on track.

In the end, mindful decision making in health and wellbeing is not flawlessness; it is consciousness and aim. So by listening to your body, eliminating noise, and then expanding on thought and care in your decision making process well then, you build a healthy process, a health experience specific to you. With mindfulness, health-oriented choices shift from being dreaded chores to being acts of self-love and development, helping you live a more colourful and harmonious life!

Lifestyle & Environmental Choices

Every decision we make on a day to day basis, from our habitual routines to what we purchase, it does not only affect our personal lives but also the environment surrounding us. Mindful lifestyle and environmental choices are choices that are made by being aware of whether our actions in fact represent our values and the world we want to live in. If we can be intentional and responsible with these choices, it will allow us to build a life that embodies our internal priorities while also serving a positive purpose at a larger scale.

In daily habits, choosing mindfully starts with the awareness of the routines that define our lives. Most of these habits are on autopilot mode, out of convenience or societal pressure rather than purposeful intent. Mindfulness invites us to pause and ask: Do our routines serve us well? Or do they need revision? For example, when you wake up, checking your phone. Does it feel like a pep start for the day or it breeds anxiety and distraction? By assessing such habits, you can swap unconscious habits with movements that can add even more equilibrium and joy into your life.

Making choices mindfully also means how we consume. Our consumer culture makes getting things easy without considering whether we need them or what impact they will have. Mindfulness creates a move away from spontaneous purchasing and into purposeful purchasing. Ask yourself if that purchase will really add to your life or if it is an impulse buy before purchasing an item. Focusing on its quality, durability, and the efforts and resources needed to produce it. This practice not only serves you to minimize your baggage in life but also where you are compelled to function in sync with sustainability.

A third example of thoughtful decision-making is in relation to impact on the environment. Whether it be food, clothing, or household items, we are having a footprint on the planet with every product we utilize. Awareness to the interconnections is the starting point of behaving in an environmentally friendly manner. You may start with making small changes in your lifestyle, such as eliminating single-use plastics, purchasing local produce or upgrading to energy-efficient appliances. This is important because every decision adds up to a larger scale effort that changes the world!

Mindfulness in our environmental choices can also mean reimagining waste. It has been demonstrated that doing something as simple as recycling, composting, or repurposing items alleviates pressure on natural resources and encourages a sense of stewardship. Moreover, engaging in activities such as meal preps to reduce food wastage or carrying cloth bags and reusable water bottles not only fosters sustainability but also makes life easier. Such lifestyle choices and habits are not only helpful for the environment but also create a sense of duty and intention in your actions!

The first step in making environmentally conscious decisions is realizing that perfection is not the objective. Global issues can be daunting, it reminds the mindfulness librarian, but we must always make the effort to pay attention to the matters that we are able to change. Even simple, regular actions — such as cycling rather than driving on short journeys, buying from ethical firms, or reducing one is power consumption — produces a big impact in the extensive run. Sustaining these efforts without getting discouraged comes from embracing progress and not perfection.

You need not make radical changes in your lifestyle to intervene with mindfulness. Work backwards — notice how your choices reflect your values and how that choice makes you/family home feel. As an example, if you are focused on health and sustainability, you may decide to prepare any dishes from whole plant based raw ingredients instead of processed foods. You want to support local artisans and businesses if community and connection means anything to you.

It encourages you to make these decisions from a place of gratitude and mindfulness. Consider the time, money, and energy that goes into the products and services you use. Even something as seemingly straightforward as a cup of coffee requires many different people and natural resources. This understanding reminds you to appreciate what you have and influence you towards actions that give back to the Earth and to mankind.

Mindful lifestyle and environmental choices come down to living in alignment with your own values and the greater world. Living intentionally through your daily choices and minimizing your impact encompasses a lifestyle that serves not only yourself, but also, the collective good of Earth. Every mindful choice, even the smallest, is a testament to a more conscious, intentional lifestyle that leads to a better tomorrow for you and the planet.

9

Embracing a Life of Clarity and Presence

You've been mindful about it and have taken a conscious approach to how you have grown and evolved. While going through this, you have learned practices and insights to help you respond to life with more clarity and presence. You have discovered eliminating the impact emotions and outside pressures have on your choices, and fostering awareness in daily habits, relationships and health; tools that allow you to live more authentically, with intention and purpose.

Mindfulness is about making space between what is demanded of you in the moment and your response so that you can respond to the situation instead of reacting mindlessly. This journey has taught you to discern between intuition and fear; how to cope with stress, how to resolve conflicts (empathetically and non-reactively). You've accepted the unknown, trusted your decision-making process, and chosen things that are aligned with your values. From career to finances to relationships to health to the environment—every choice represents a commitment to presence and purpose; their practices have helped you navigate these complex areas.

This practice of mindful decision-making will be sustainable and long-lasting only when we make it a part of our daily life. This begins with consistency. Establishing practices like meditation, journaling, or mindful breathing offer a base which will make it easier to stop, think and act with intention. It only takes a handful of minutes each day to implement these practices in your life and begin making fundamental shifts in your decision-making process. With time, mindfulness becomes less of an activity and more of a state of being that guides your life through both the trivial as well as the pivotal moments of your life.

To carry this journey forward, be adaptable. Naturally life is also changing, and your mindfulness practice should also change. Some days, a proper meditation will feel impossible, but a mindful walk or a stop to follow your breath can be the ground you need. The secret lies in meeting yourself where you are, gently and with lots of flexibility.

And another piece is reflection! Continually checking back in with yourself as to whether your decisions, behaviors, and habits are still in alignment with your values and goals. That awareness will keep you in alignment with your purpose so that whatever you do, you are doing with conscious intentions. Reflecting also allows you to acknowledge your progress—celebrating how you've grown, but recognizing where you still need to explore.

At last, create a network of accountability. When you share your mindfulness journey with others — in writing, conversation or group meditation, for example — you strengthen your own commitment while creating stronger connections with others. The advice of a helpful network can open your eyes to new ideas and provide motivation when you need it most.

Having purpose and being clear is about doing the best with the information we have at any one time. Related: It's Less About Each Moment, More About Being Present, Learning and Making The Most Of Things Life is full of choices, big and small and this is the reminder that every choice is a chance to live in alignment with your values and grow into the person you want to be. Even wrong turns and hesitation serve well, slinging you on the path to an ever more stable and familiar you.

And as you persevere and advance, know that being mindful is not the destination but an ongoing practice. With each mindful breath, every hesitation before an action, and every moment of kindness toward yourself and others contributes to a full life. The clarity and presence born of a mindfulness practice extend far beyond the individual, benefiting not only yourself but also the people around you.

By accepting this journey, you are opting for a life of meaning, facing the challenges bravely & relishing the moment. Such a life is the core of mindfulness; a life based on clarity ideologically, a life lived by purpose, and a life recognized that every single choice has the potential to change your life.

About the Author

Evangeline Brooks is a celebrated author and thought leader in the fields of mindfulness, personal growth, and philosophical exploration. With a profound ability to distill complex concepts into accessible wisdom, she has captivated readers around the world. Her previous works, The Art of Being Happy: A Philosophical Exploration, Meditation and the Path to Self-Discovery: Connecting with Your True Essence, and The Art of Letting Go: Overcoming Ego and Letting Go, have established her as a trusted voice for those seeking clarity and meaning in life.

In her latest book, Pause and Decide: A Mindful Approach to Everyday Decisions, Brooks deepens her exploration of mindfulness, offering practical strategies to navigate life's choices with grace and intention. Drawing on her extensive understanding of meditation, psychology, and philosophy, she empowers readers to embrace a more present and purpose-driven way of living.

Known for her transformative insights and empathetic writing style, Evangeline Brooks continues to inspire readers to cultivate inner peace, resilience, and authenticity in an ever-changing world.

Milton Keynes UK
Ingram Content Group UK Ltd.
UKHW022022071224
452128UK00001B/113